RAND NATIONAL DEFENSE RESEARCH INSTITUTE

T0308614

Hazing in the U.S. Armed Forces

Recommendations for Hazing Prevention Policy and Practice

Kirsten M. Keller, Miriam Matthews, Kimberly Curry Hall,
William Marcellino, Jacqueline A. Mauro, Nelson Lim

Prepared for the Office of the Secretary of Defense

Approved for public release; distribution unlimited

For more information on this publication, visit www.rand.org/t/rr/941

Library of Congress Cataloging-in-Publication Data

Keller, Kirsten M.
Hazing in the U.S. Armed Forces : recommendations for hazing prevention policy and practice / Kirsten M. Keller, Miriam Matthews, Kimberly Curry Hall, William Marcellino, Jacqueline A. Mauro, Nelson Lim.
pages cm
Includes bibliographical references.
ISBN 978-0-8330-9027-0 (pbk. : alk. paper)
1. United States—Armed Forces—Military life. 2. Bullying—United States. 3. Hazing—United States—Government policy. 4. Military offenses—United States. 5. Soldiers—United States—Social conditions. I. Title. II. Title: Recommendations for hazing prevention policy and practice.
U766.K44 2015
355.6'1--dc23 2015023798

Published by the RAND Corporation, Santa Monica, Calif.

Preface

Initiation activities have long been part of U.S. military culture as a way to mark significant transitions, status changes, and group membership. However, along with these activities have often come acts of hazing, in which individuals are subjected to abusive and harmful treatment. In recent years, extreme cases of alleged hazing have led to the high-profile deaths of several service members, resulting in renewed interest from the public and Congress in seeing these hazing rituals eliminated from military culture.

In 2012, to help build a more-systematic approach to hazing prevention and response, the Office of the Secretary of Defense had the Office of Diversity Management and Equal Opportunity form a working group composed of representatives from each of the services to address hazing. The Office of Diversity Management and Equal Opportunity then asked RAND to support the working group's efforts by examining and providing recommendations on current hazing prevention policy and practices across the services. RAND was asked to address the following objectives:

- Determine whether the 1997 definition of hazing is relevant or should be refined to better track hazing incidents across the armed forces.
- Identify practices to prevent and respond to incidents of hazing.
- Examine the feasibility of and key data elements needed for a comprehensive hazing incident database.

In this report, we address ways to improve the armed forces' definition of hazing, the effects of and motivations for hazing, how the armed forces can prevent and respond to hazing, and how the armed forces can improve the tracking of hazing incidents.

This report should be of interest to policymakers responsible for hazing prevention and response both within the military and the public. This research was sponsored by the Office of Diversity Management and Equal Opportunity within the Office of the Under Secretary of Defense for Personnel and Readiness and was conducted within the Forces and Resources Policy Center of the RAND National Defense Research Institute, a federally funded research and development center sponsored by the Office of the Secretary of Defense, the Joint Staff, the Unified Combatant Commands, the Navy, the Marine Corps, the defense agencies, and the defense Intelligence Community under contract number W91WAW-12-C-0030.

For more information on the RAND Forces and Resources Policy Center, see http://www.rand.org/nsrd/ndri/centers/frp.html or contact the Center director (contact information provided on the web page).

Contents

Tables

Summary

Initiation activities have long been part of U.S. military culture as a way to mark significant transitions, status changes, and group membership. However, along with these activities have often come acts of hazing, in which individuals were subjected to abusive and harmful treatment that went beyond sanctioned ceremonies. In recent years, extreme cases of alleged hazing have led to the high-profile deaths of several service members, resulting in renewed interest from the public and Congress in seeing these hazing rituals eliminated from military culture.

In 2012, to help build a more-systematic approach to hazing prevention and response, the Office of the Secretary of Defense had the Office of Diversity Management and Equal Opportunity form a working group composed of representatives from each of the services to address hazing. The Office of Diversity Management and Equal Opportunity then asked RAND to support the working group's efforts by examining and providing recommendations on current hazing prevention policy and practices across the services. RAND was asked to address the following objectives:

- Determine whether the 1997 definition of hazing is relevant or should be refined to better track hazing incidents across the armed forces.
- Identify practices to prevent and respond to incidents of hazing.
- Examine the feasibility of and key data elements needed for a comprehensive hazing incident database.

In this report, we address ways to improve the armed forces' definition of hazing, the effects of and motivations for hazing, how the armed forces can prevent and respond to hazing, and how the armed forces can improve the tracking of hazing incidents.

Analytical Approach

To better understand current hazing-related policies and practices, RAND reviewed current Department of Defense (DoD) and service policy documents and held policy discussions with individuals responsible for hazing prevention from each of the services. This review included examining the services' current methods for tracking hazing incidents and existing hazing prevention education and training materials. We also reviewed the scientific literature and interviewed leading hazing prevention experts to better understand how to define hazing, the root causes of hazing, and effective hazing prevention and response practices that may be applicable to the DoD environment. Finally, to examine the feasibility of creating a comprehensive DoD-wide hazing incident database, we reviewed the development and operation of several existing DoD-wide databases that could serve as examples for the creation and implementation of a DoD-wide hazing incident database.

Defining Hazing

Confusion persists regarding what actions constitute hazing and what do not. Although DoD and the services, along with multiple states, organizations, and research efforts, have established their own definitions of hazing, there are inconsistencies across these definitions, which may contribute to this confusion.

A well-understood and well-publicized definition of hazing in the military is needed. DoD developed its own definition of hazing in 1997, which each of the military services has adopted. However, each service has slightly modified the definition and may present different definitions of hazing during training, as discussed in Chapter Four. DoD's current definition is as follows:

> Hazing is defined as any conduct whereby a military member or members, regardless of service or rank, without proper authority causes another military member or members, regardless of service or rank, to suffer or be exposed to any activity which is cruel, abusive, humiliating, oppressive, demeaning, or harmful. Soliciting or coercing another to perpetrate any such activity is also considered hazing. Hazing need not involve physical contact among or between military members; it can be verbal or psychological in nature. Actual or implied consent to acts of hazing does not eliminate the culpability of the perpetrator.
>
> The above definition can include, but is not limited to, the following: playing abusive tricks; threatening or offering violence or bodily harm to another; striking; branding; tattooing; shaving; greasing; painting; "pinning," "tacking on," "blood wings"; or forcing or requiring consumption of food, alcohol, drugs, or any other substance (Cohen, 1997).

As recommended by scholars (e.g., Crow and Rosner, 2002; Pelletier, 2002), this definition notes that hazing can be psychological and need not involve physical contact. It also establishes that the consent of the victim does not eliminate the culpability of hazers and provides examples of hazing activities that may be prevalent in the military context.

However, this definition also has some limitations. For example, it appears to absolve individuals of responsibility for hazing if the acts have been approved by an authority figure and that it may be overly broad.

We recommend the following improvements to DoD's definition of hazing:[1]

---

1 Since completion of this study, the Hazing Review Team has drafted a revised definition for hazing which incorporates many of these recommendations. The revised definition will be included in new DoD hazing policy.

- Include qualities that are distinctive to hazing, to distinguish it from other types of abuse and mistreatment. For example, it should be noted that hazing activities are often performed as part of initiations, to maintain group membership, or as part of a change in status or position within a group.
- To address authority-approved hazing, clarify the role of authority figures and the individual's responsibility. This will help eliminate ambiguity about the culpability of those who perform acts of authority-sanctioned hazing.
- Consider the use of more objective terms in describing harm, such as "psychological injury" or "extreme mental stress." These may be used in addition to, or as alternatives to, "humiliating" or "demeaning." The terms used should be clear and specific about the psychological consequences of interest.
- Ensure that the list of examples is based on hazing acts considered to be prevalent within the military today. These could be drawn from recently prosecuted or reported hazing acts or based on perceptions of prevalence from service members. These examples can also be used to differentiate hazing from sanctioned rituals and training exercises. For service-specific policies or training, the individual services may also want to tailor the examples to the acts performed most often in the particular service.

The Effects of and Motivations for Hazing

Hazing is often described as involving abuse of potential and new members of a group (it may also include some maltreatment of current members) by more-senior individuals with the goal of bringing the new members into the group. Hazing is common across different countries, cultures, and societies, and hazing or similar ritualistic behaviors have been practiced for centuries (Cimino, 2011; Sosis, 2004). Proponents of hazing argue that acts of hazing or harsh initiation rituals contribute to increased liking of, commitment to, and cohesion within the group. However, evidence for these different effects is mixed, and research and reports demonstrate that hazing can lead to physical and psychological injuries among hazees (Finkel, 2002). Research suggests that individuals endure hazing to signal their commitment to group members and, thus, receive the benefits of group membership. In addition, hazers may use hazing to eliminate free riders (those who take benefits of group membership without paying costs for these benefits) and to maintain power differentials within the group.

The military is a hierarchical organization in which individuals operate as highly cooperative teams, often in high-risk environments. Identifying acts of hazing in this environment may be difficult. Thus, broad consideration of the cognitive processes and attitudes that cause people to haze others or to endure being hazed may assist in better understanding and addressing hazing among the armed forces.

Preventing and Responding to Hazing in the Armed Forces

Multiple sources have identified potential avenues for preventing and responding to hazing within an organization, school, or community; however, comprehensive antihazing efforts have not been evaluated systematically. Subject-matter experts we spoke to and literature we reviewed note that antihazing efforts can be implemented at the organizational level and at the personal level and that comprehensive antihazing initiatives include efforts at both levels.

Our analysis of current service antihazing training and education materials showed variation among the services in standardization and frequency of the antihazing training provided to service members. For example, only some services provided annual training, and only some provided training specifically directed toward leaders. In terms of the training content, most of the services focus on providing facts and information that may increase knowledge about hazing but do not address attitudes, skills, or behaviors. Finally, most of the service training appears to encourage passive learning, which can be helpful for rapid communication of a large amount of information. However, use of instructor-led discussion, which may encourage greater active learning, varies across the services, with the Army and Navy training materials showing the strongest evidence of use of this technique.

As a first step in developing a more-systematic response to hazing prevention, the armed forces may wish to conduct a needs assessment, including a local analysis that reviews the scope of hazing and initiation activities, factors that contribute to or reduce the risk of hazing within the local context, and the resources that are currently available or that may be needed to facilitate a more-effective approach to hazing elimination. In addition, the desired end results of an antihazing program must be specified, and a time frame for implementation and assessment of effects should be established.

We identified several broad areas that should be addressed within the armed forces' antihazing prevention and response efforts:

- at the organization level, antihazing programs should
  - Communicate antihazing policies and consequences.
  - Hold leaders accountable for hazing prevention and swift enforcement of punishment for hazing.
  - Ensure that there are options for reporting anonymously and outside the chain of command.
  - Maintain accurate records of hazing allegations or incidents.
  - Assign an office to provide service-level oversight.
- at the individual level, antihazing programs should
  - Be comprehensive and continuous.
  - Include a training sequence that increases knowledge, influences attitudes and perceptions, and changes or develops behaviors and skills.
  - Teach leaders how to identify and address hazing.
  - Incorporate active learning techniques.

Understanding the Prevalence and Characteristics of Hazing Incidents

One key limitation of DoD's efforts to combat hazing is the lack of a good sense of the scope of the hazing problem across DoD because very few data have been collected or maintained on military hazing. To effectively address hazing in the military, DoD and the services need to understand the scope of hazing within their ranks. We reviewed current hazing incident tracking methods across DoD, assessed the feasibility of a potential DoD-wide hazing database, and identified ways that the armed forces can improve the tracking of hazing incidents.

We reviewed the services' current systems for tracking hazing incidents using six characteristics. As Table S.1 shows, none of the systems incorporates all six characteristics. Furthermore, no service has a standalone database to track hazing. All current and pending tracking methods in the armed forces have involved adding hazing to an existing database originally developed for a different purpose.

Given the current lack of uniformity in tracking hazing incidents at the service level, we explored the feasibility of creating a comprehensive hazing database at the DoD level that would incorporate hazing incident data from each of the services. The Defense Sexual Assault

Table S.1
Characteristics of Current Service Tracking Methods

Characteristic	Army[a]	Navy	Marine Corps	Coast Guard
The system is exclusively for hazing				
Hazing is a standalone category in the database	✓	✓	✓	✓
The system tracks bullying separately	✓			
The system tracks anonymous reports	✓	✓		
The system tracks initial report to final disposition	✓	✓	✓	
The system tracks all allegations of hazing	✓	✓	✓	

NOTE: The Air Force and U.S. National Guard were not included in this assessment because they do not formally track hazing incidents.

[a] Our assessment of Army hazing incident tracking methods was based on the planned tracking system that is currently under development.

Incident Database and the Recovery Coordination Program Support Solution database, two databases that track data at the DoD level and have relevant but limited content, offer some best practices for a possible DoD-wide hazing database. Ultimately, however, we recommend leveraging existing service-level databases rather than developing a new, DoD-level database at this time. Existing service systems could be modified to ensure that uniform data elements are tracked across the services. This would avoid duplication of effort at the DoD level and minimize additional time and resource requirements. Additionally, DoD does not currently have a clear understanding of the scope of the hazing problem. Once the department has a clear definition of hazing and is able to uniformly track hazing incidents and better assess scope, it can then better determine whether to invest in a DoD-wide database system or whether service-level tracking remains sufficient.

From the interviews with hazing experts in academia and service representatives from the Hazing Review Team, we also identified the following key elements for tracking that DoD should consider establishing

- demographics of victim(s) and alleged perpetrator(s)
- location type (e.g., ship or shore)
- characteristics of hazing incident circumstances (e.g., whether the incident stemmed from a ceremony, whether alcohol was involved)
- types of behaviors involved to use as examples for training (e.g., physical, verbal, or psychological)
- severity of the hazing incident (e.g., subtle versus violent; mild, moderate, or severe)
- investigative process elements (e.g., length of time for investigation; whether the allegation was substantiated; outcome of the report, including punishment).

Finally, to complement any formal tracking system, we also recommend that DoD survey the force to obtain a more-comprehensive assessment of hazing that is representative of the entire force:

- Survey participation should be confidential or anonymous to ensure that respondents feel they can be open and honest when answering the survey questions.
- Survey items should not use the term *hazing* to ask specifically about experiences. There is no clear understanding of what hazing includes, and there is also potential for bias—for instance, some may view hazing as a positive, "rite of passage" activity.
- Rather than reference hazing specifically, survey items should use example behaviors, which will promote more-reliable responses. The example behaviors for inclusion in the survey measure should be based on behaviors that have been identified as the most prevalent types of hazing in the services. Data on these behaviors can be collected from such sources as interviews, focus groups, and analysis of reported incidents.
- DoD should also consider including survey items related to attitudes toward hazing.

Conclusion

Rites of passage and initiation rituals have long been part of U.S. military culture. However, along with these activities have often come acts of hazing, in which individuals are subjected to abusive treatment that goes beyond sanctioned ceremonies in an effort to solidify commitment to the group and/or its structure. In recent years, more-extreme cases of hazing have led to the high-profile deaths of several service members, resulting in renewed interest from the public and Congress in eliminating these hazing rituals from military culture. The recommendations documented in this report provide a foundation for the DoD to begin to develop a more-systematic approach to preventing and responding to hazing across the armed forces.

Acknowledgements

We are grateful to the many people who were involved in this research. In particular, we would like to thank our project sponsor, Clarence Johnson, Director of the Office of Diversity Management and Equal Opportunity (Office of the Under Secretary of Defense for Personnel and Readiness), for his support. We also benefited greatly from the guidance and feedback of our project monitors, Stephanie Miller and Beatrice Bernfeld. This work also would not have been possible without the support of and participation from members of the DoD Hazing Review Team, who provided us with critical information regarding current service policies and practices. We are also thankful to the insights provided by the following academic scholars and hazing prevention experts we interviewed: Hank Nuwer, Jennifer Waldron, Judy Van Raalte, Caroline Keating, Mary Madden, R. Brian Crow, Charles Hall, Susan Lipkins, and Norm Pollard. We would also like to thank Jennifer Lewis and John Winkler, the associate director and director of the Forces and Resources Policy Center of the RAND National Defense Research Institute, for their feedback throughout this project. We are also thankful to Bernard Rostker, a RAND colleague and former Under Secretary of Defense for Personnel and Readiness, who served as a dedicated reviewer for this project, providing critical review of the findings and recommendations contained within this report. His comments greatly contributed to improving the quality of this work. We also thank Andrew Morral, another RAND colleague and principal investigator on the 2014 RAND Military Workplace Study, for his constructive review of this report. Finally, the report benefited from the work of Julie Ann Tajiri, who provided administrative support, and James Torr, who helped write the summary and provide overall editorial assistance.

Abbreviations

CGIS	Coast Guard Investigative Service
DASH	Discrimination and Sexual Harassment
DEOCS	DEOMI Organizational Climate Survey
DEOMI	Defense Equal Opportunity Management Institute
DoD	Department of Defense
DMDC	Defense Manpower Data Center
DSAID	Defense Sexual Assault Incident Database
EOA	Equal Opportunity Adivsor
EORS	Equal Opportunity Reporting System
FAMU	Florida A&M University
FIPG	Fraternity Insurance Protection Group
FY	fiscal year
GAO	U.S. Government Accountability Office
IG	Inspector General
MEONet	Military Equal Opportunity Network
NCAA	National Collegiate Athletic Association
NDAA	National Defense Authorization Act

OSD	Office of the Secretary of Defense
RCP-SS	Recovery Coordination Program Support Solution
SAPR	Sexual Assault Prevention and Response
SAPRO	Sexual Assault and Prevention Office
UCMJ	Uniform Code of Military Justice
USMC	U.S. Marine Corps

CHAPTER ONE

Introduction

Initiation activities have long been part of U.S. military culture as a way to mark significant transitions, status changes, and group membership. However, along with these activities have also come acts of hazing in which individuals are subjected to abusive and harmful treatment that goes beyond sanctioned ceremonies (Nuwer, 2004). These acts of hazing have ranged from initiation rituals into a new rank, such as "blood pinning" (i.e., pins on the insignia are driven into the flesh of the person being promoted), to tests of newcomers' commitment to the group through extended verbal and physical abuse. In recent years, more extreme cases of alleged hazing have led to the deaths of several service members, resulting in renewed interest from the public and Congress in eliminating these hazing rituals from military culture. To this end, the Fiscal Year (FY) 2013 National Defense Authorization Act (NDAA) required an initial report from each of the service secretaries to the House and Senate Armed Services Committees in 2013 regarding each service's efforts to address hazing.

The Department of Defense (DoD) has noted that hazing is unacceptable in the military services. In 1997, the Secretary of Defense provided the following statement on how hazing should be treated in the services:

> Treating each other with dignity and respect is essential to morale, operational readiness, and mission accomplishment. Hazing is contrary to these goals. Hazing must not be allowed to occur; and when it does, action should be prompt and effective—not

only to deal with the incident, but also to prevent future occurrences. (Cohen, 1997)

However, at the time of this research, no uniform definition of hazing was widely used across the services, and hazing was not an enumerated offense under the Uniform Code of Military Justice (UCMJ), making incident reporting and tracking difficult. In addition, very few data have been collected or maintained on military hazing, and robust research on hazing in the armed forces is sparse and dated (see U.S. Government Accountability Office [GAO], 1992).

Therefore, in 2012, to help build a more-systematic approach to hazing prevention and response, the Office of the Secretary of Defense (OSD) asked the OSD Office of Diversity Management and Equal Opportunity to form a Hazing Review Team with representatives of each of the services. The OSD Office of Diversity Management and Equal Opportunity then asked RAND to support the team's efforts by examining current hazing prevention policy and practices across the services and providing recommendations on how to modify these policies and practices to better align them with scientific literature on effectively addressing hazing.

Study Tasks and Analytical Approach

In support of the efforts of the Hazing Review Team, RAND was asked to

- determine whether the 1997 definition of hazing is relevant or should be refined to better track hazing incidents across the armed forces
- identify best practices to prevent and respond to incidents of hazing
- examine the feasibility of and key data elements needed for a comprehensive hazing incident database.

Accordingly, we gathered information from a variety of sources (see Appendix A for more detail on our methodology):

- First, to better understand current hazing related policies and practices, we reviewed current DoD and service policy documents and discussed these policies with representatives from each of the services who are responsible for hazing prevention. This review included examining the services' current methods of tracking hazing incidents and existing hazing prevention education and training materials.
- Second, we reviewed the scientific literature and interviewed leading hazing researchers and prevention experts to better understand how to define hazing, the root causes of hazing, and effective hazing prevention and response practices that may be applicable to the DoD environment.
- Finally, to examine the feasibility of creating a comprehensive DoD-wide hazing incident database, we reviewed the development and operation of several existing DoD-wide databases that could serve as examples for the creation and implementation of a DoD-wide hazing incident database.

One key limitation of DoD's efforts to combat hazing is the lack of a good sense of the scope of the hazing problem across DoD because very few data have been collected or maintained on military hazing. At the initiation of the project, we were given a fourth task, to examine recent hazing incident records within the military (e.g., court-martial reports, records of nonjudicial punishment) and to identify key factors associated with these incidents. However, as will be discussed later, the services do not currently track hazing incidents systematically and have only recently begun developing more-robust tracking methods. Therefore, we were not able to determine the true number or even the scope of hazing incidents that may exist across the services, let alone key factors associated with different types of hazing incidents. In addition, no single data repository documents even the known cases of hazing that appear in court-martial records or are documented in nonjudicial punishment records, making a more-detailed analysis impossible. However, we were able to examine current research on why hazing occurs (see Chapter Three) and developed an initial taxonomy of military hazing activities using several example published hazing incidents.

To better tailor the prevention and response efforts described in this report, it will be critical for DoD to examine hazing activities across the services more thoroughly in the future. Although it was outside the scope of the current study, this examination should also include gaining a better understanding of service members' knowledge about, attitudes on, and experiences of hazing.

Organization of the Report

The remaining chapters in this report document our study findings and recommendations. In Chapter Two, we first review various definitions of hazing that exist in academia and state laws, then discuss whether the 1997 DoD definition of hazing should be refined. Chapter Three provides information on the effects of and motivations for hazing, including a discussion of why hazing may be particularly ingrained in military culture. The chapter also presents a theoretical taxonomy of examples of military hazing incidents, with information from news reports and case studies. Chapter Four describes our findings and our recommendations for practices to prevent and respond to incidents of hazing within the military. Chapter Five describes current service systems for tracking hazing incidents and examines the feasibility of creating a comprehensive DoD-wide hazing incident database. Finally, Chapter Six presents our overall conclusions and final recommendations.

The report also includes a number of appendixes. Appendix A details the study's methodological approach for addressing each research task. Appendix B provides an in-depth description of an institutional hazing reform program that Florida A&M University (FAMU) undertook following the 2011 hazing-related death of drum major Robert Champion. Appendix C details our coding of service hazing-relevant training materials discussed in Chapter Four.

CHAPTER TWO

Defining Hazing

Without a common, well-understood definition, it may be difficult to identify acts of hazing, which prevents development of a consistent report of hazing incidents. The term *hazing* has different meanings for different people, and confusion persists about which actions constitute hazing and which do not. Although multiple states, organizations, and research efforts have established their own definitions of hazing, there are inconsistencies across these definitions, which may contribute to persistent uncertainty about hazing. In the military, there are multiple activities that service members may have difficulty differentiating from hazing. To assist them in recognizing incidents of hazing, service members need a well-understood and well-publicized definition of hazing in the military. Notably, such a definition will not, by itself, reduce confusion regarding hazing. Rather, education regarding the definition and which actions constitute hazing is also needed, as discussed in Chapter Four.

No single definition of hazing has received widespread support across both military and nonmilitary contexts. DoD developed its own definition of hazing in 1997, which each of the military services has adopted, but with slight modifications:

> Hazing is defined as any conduct whereby a military member or members, regardless of service or rank, without proper authority causes another military member or members, regardless of service or rank, to suffer or be exposed to any activity which is cruel, abusive, humiliating, oppressive, demeaning, or harmful. Soliciting or coercing another to perpetrate any such activity is also con-

> sidered hazing. Hazing need not involve physical contact among or between military members; it can be verbal or psychological in nature. Actual or implied consent to acts of hazing does not eliminate the culpability of the perpetrator.
>
> The above definition can include, but is not limited to, the following: playing abusive tricks; threatening or offering violence or bodily harm to another; striking; branding; tattooing; shaving; greasing; painting; "pinning," "tacking on," "blood wings"; or forcing or requiring consumption of food, alcohol, drugs, or any other substance. (Cohen, 1997)

In a 2013 report to Congress assessing hazing in the armed forces, however, DoD expressed concern that this definition may be overly broad, making incident reporting and tracking difficult.

This chapter reviews research on individual knowledge of hazing and outlines recommended key components of hazing definitions. The chapter draws from information obtained from the scientific literature on hazing and related topics and reviews hazing definitions contained in laws and relevant organizational policies (e.g., schools, universities, and paramilitary organizations, such as police departments). Building from this information, the chapter then assesses the 1997 DoD definition of hazing and provides recommendations for improving the definition.

Knowledge of Hazing

Several studies have explored individual understanding of and ability to identify acts of hazing. Overall, this research suggests that those who have experienced hazing are often not aware that they were hazed, and those who conducted hazing are often not aware that their actions are illegal in most states. For example, a large study of hazing among U.S. college students found that, although 55 percent of college students who were affiliated with an organization or sports team identified that that they had experienced at least one act that had been previously identified as constituting hazing, 91 percent of these students did not perceive the experienced act(s) as hazing (Allan and Madden, 2008). This gap between the experience and identification of hazing appears to be due in part to student misunderstanding and inability to clearly define hazing. Similarly, research that has focused on U.S. high school students (Hoover and Pollard, 2000), athletes at National Collegiate Athletic Association (NCAA) schools (Hoover, 1999), and members of diverse college student organizations (Ellsworth, 2004) has also shown a widespread inability among students to differentiate acts that constitute hazing from those that do not.

Students also appear to be unaware of the legal implications of hazing. In research conducted with members of fraternities and sororities, participants did not know that hazing, as defined by different states, is a criminal act in most states and were unaware of statutes prohibiting hazing (Montague et al., 2008). Further, many participants felt that hazing should continue, as long as it did not surpass a threshold of acceptable behavior. However, they were not able to explain what this threshold of acceptable hazing behavior was.

Notably, confusion and uncertainty about hazing are not limited to high school and college students. Rather, staff and personnel at these institutions also lack consensus on hazing. For example, focus groups that included university coaches and administrators could not agree on a definition of hazing (Crow and Macintosh, 2009). This lack of consensus on a single definition of hazing appears due in part to differences in perceptions of whether activities were harmless or emotionally harmful and, similarly, whether activities were part of acceptable team initiations or were demeaning acts that may be considered hazing. Without a clear definition of hazing and exemplars of activities that clearly constitute hazing, there is a great deal of room for subjectivity in assessment of which actions may be identified as hazing, and this subjectivity may contribute to subsequent disagreement and confusion regarding hazing (Pelletier, 2002).

Military Hazing Knowledge

Although several studies have assessed hazing knowledge among those who are not affiliated with the military, assessment of knowledge about what constitutes hazing within the military is relatively limited.

Research that does exist in this area has focused on hazing at the military service academies. For example, a report of hazing activities at the military service academies conducted by the GAO (1992) commented on the difficulty that students have in differentiating military service academy training from hazing.

Students in their first year at the academies, known as fourth-class cadets, go through rigorous training throughout most of the year. Multiple uncomfortable and stress-inducing traditions and customs have been incorporated into this first-year training. The GAO (1992) assessment of cadet ability to differentiate legitimate indoctrination from acts of hazing highlighted an apparent lack of clarity between these acts. Although the military academies had definitions of and regulations on hazing, cadets did not understand these definitions. Specifically, cadets had difficulty differentiating between sanctioned actions that serve legitimate training functions or that are harmless and those that constitute hazing. For example, students at the U.S. Naval Academy did not demonstrate clear understanding of the academy's hazing definition. After further explanation, they indicated awareness that acts that constituted hazing, as defined by the academy, had occurred during their tenure.

Subsequent research has built on the 1992 GAO assessment of hazing in the academies (see Pershing, 2006). This research reassessed the GAO data and drew on interviews conducted in 1994 with officers who graduated from the U.S. Naval Academy in 1992 or 1993. Among other things, this research highlighted the disparity between the small number of hazing charges at the U.S. Naval Academy and the much greater number of surveyed self-reports of hazing. One hypothesized reason for this disparity was uncertainty about whether an experienced act was training or hazing. Interviews with graduates demonstrated the apparent confusion between these two categories of actions. For example, one officer noted "You don't have any time to yourself during plebe year because you're hazed all year. Well, I don't know if I'd call it hazing. It's also training. You have responsibilities you have to do for the upperclassmen like learning things about the military and strategy" (Pershing, 2006, p. 485). It is likely that similar confusion exists at the other service academies. However, we are not aware of comparable research involving graduates of the other military service academies.

We could also not find comprehensive research involving empirical assessment of hazing knowledge among U.S. military personnel who are not at the military service academies. However, we did find research suggesting that difficulty in identifying and describing hazing is an issue in militaries across nations. For example, research conducted with conscripts of the Norwegian Army demonstrated that they were unable to clearly differentiate acts of hazing from other actions, such as acts of bullying (Ostvik and Rudmin, 2001). Research assessing the Canadian Airborne Regiment also suggests a difficulty in differentiating acceptable behaviors to promote group bonding from acts of hazing (Winslow, 1999). Thus, those in the military may have particular difficulty defining and identifying acts of hazing because of ambiguity about which activities are and are not sanctioned. Further, there is the potential for sanctioned activities to transition into or include activities that are unsanctioned and would constitute hazing. This suggests that the armed forces need to review sanctioned activities, referencing their hazing definition, to ensure sanctioned actions do not constitute hazing and carefully monitor these sanctioned events and actions.

Hazing Definitions

Without assistance, hazing is a difficult construct for individuals to identify and describe. Various people may have a diversity of ways in which they conceptualize hazing. Therefore, no common understanding of hazing exists. However, establishment, publication, and discussion of a clear definition of hazing in the military may assist in reducing confusion among those in the armed forces and may improve individual ability to identify specific acts of hazing. As noted earlier, midshipmen who received an explanation of the U.S. Naval Academy's definition of hazing then indicated that they were aware of acts of hazing that occurred during their tenure (GAO, 1992). Additional research has also demonstrated that individuals are better able to identify acts of hazing after receiving a definition. Further, research has found that use of a definition that includes a list of specific examples of hazing helps participants identify hazing activities better than a definition that simply describes the construct (Kittle, 2012).[1]

Commonalities Across Hazing Definitions and Statutes

Although there is a great deal of variability across definitions of hazing, they have some common themes. These themes highlight characteristics that differentiate hazing from other acts of abuse or mistreatment. For example, hazing is often described as a form of harassment that is performed by one cohort of senior individuals against another cohort (Ostvik and Rudmin, 2001). The cohort being hazed typically consists of either newcomers to the group or of subordinate (i.e., lower-ranking) individuals within the group. Although newcomers and subordinates might abuse or act aggressively toward seniors or superiors, such acts would not technically constitute hazing.

In addition, acts of hazing have ritualistic, or traditional, components. For example, scholars have noted that hazing actions tend to occur in a ceremonial context (Cimino, 2011). In the case of the military, research at the military academies found that acts of hazing are ritualized and passed down over generations, contributing to confusion over whether these acts are sanctioned traditions or illegal actions (Pershing, 2006). In contrast, other acts of abuse or aggression are unconstrained and can involve novel behaviors. This demonstrates that hazing is not synonymous with other acts of abuse or mistreatment, such as bullying.

Additionally, unlike other forms of abuse or mistreatement that can continue indefinitely, hazing has a relatively clear point at which it discontinues. Although hazers may require hazees to perform embarrassing and dangerous behaviors, hazers must cease making these orders and demands at some point (Cimino, 2011). This point of discontinuation occurs when seniors or superiors believe that subordinates or newcomers have demonstrated their commitment to the group (Waldron, 2012).

---

[1] It is important to note that this research did not assess the utility of all currently used definitions of hazing, and exposure to multiple definitions may contribute to confusion.

Finally, hazing is intended to socialize individuals into a group (Ostvik and Rudmin, 2001). Those who are able to endure the hazing are eventually accepted as group members. Other acts of abuse or mistreatment, such as bullying, serve to keep individuals out of a particular group.

Critiques of Hazing Definitions and Statutes

Referencing college hazing, reports have noted that, "Inconsistent state laws and overbroad definitions of hazing in campus policies also create confusion and a lack of commitment to enforcement" (Hollmann, 2002, p. 20). Additional research on hazing statutes and definitions has outlined general limitations contained within hazing definitions (Crow and Rosner, 2002; Pelletier, 2002).

For example, many state laws limit their hazing definitions to educational institutions and students, preventing individuals who are not in that context from filing a legal case under the state's hazing statute (Crow and Rosner, 2002). This suggests that the individuals and institutions to which a hazing definition applies should be carefully considered when drafting legislation or policy. If it is unclear whether a definition applies in certain contexts, it may be difficult for some individuals to litigate or be held accountable under the hazing statute or policy.

In addition, how different definitions of hazing address the consent of an individual to be hazed varies. In some cases involving hazing, defendants have argued that the victim consented to being hazed (Pelletier, 2002). To prevent the use of this defense, some states have explicitly noted that victim consent does not establish that a particular act was not hazing.

Further, hazing definitions have also been attacked for being overly broad. Overbreadth is a particular issue for hazing definitions that address psychological, mental, or emotional harm. Specifically, as one of the most thorough previous reviews of hazing definitions noted, "Constitutional challenges [to hazing definitions] arise in the murky territory of what constitutes mental or emotional harm" (Pelletier, 2002, p. 389). Although there are many hazing cases in which there is psychological, mental, or emotional harm but not physical harm, it can be difficult to establish what constitutes harm, and there is some subjectivity in establishing that this form of harm has been done. Thus, a hazing definition needs clear and specific terms for the consequences of interest.

Also, some hazing definitions are so broad that they do not differentiate acts of hazing from other types of abuse or mistreatment, including bullying and sexual harassment. This may contribute to difficulties in identifying and reporting hazing (e.g., Ostvik and Rudmin, 2001). Specifically, ambiguity and confusion about the particular category of acts experienced may contribute to individual hesitance and disinclination to report them. Many hazing definitions also do not include example acts of hazing. Among the definitions that do include examples, the prevalence of the listed acts is often unclear. For example, a list of example acts that are rare may be of little use in clarifying what actions constitute hazing.

With these limitations in mind, the next section provides an overview of several example hazing definitions. A thorough description of all hazing definitions that different organizations, institutions, and government entities within the United States use is beyond the scope of this chapter. We therefore describe several relevant and often-cited definitions instead.

States' Definitions of Hazing

All but the following states have legislation on hazing: Alaska, Hawaii, Montana, New Mexico, South Dakota, and Wyoming. For reference purposes, Table 2.1 includes the definitions used in the states with the most military personnel: Texas, California, North Carolina, and Virginia (Office of the Deputy Assistant Secretary of Defense, 2014).

Although these definitions have several positive aspects, they also have several limitations. For example, they do not address hazing outside the context of educational institutions and students. In addition, most of the definitions do not include specific examples of hazing activities or note the qualities that are specific to hazing. Most of the definitions limit hazing to initiation or preinitiation activities, whereas hazing can also occur against individuals who are full members of the group. Some, but not all, of the definitions incorporate psychological

Table 2.1
Definitions of Hazing Used by Texas, California, North Carolina, and Virginia

Source and Definition	Comments
Texas Education Code, Section 37.151	
"Hazing" means any intentional knowing, or reckless act, occurring on or off the campus of an educational institution, by one person alone or acting with others, directed against a student that endangers the mental or physical health or safety of a student for the purpose of pledging, being initiated into, affiliating with, holding office in, or maintaining membership in any organization whose members are students at an educational institution. The term includes but is not limited to: 1. any type of physical brutality, such as whipping, beating, striking, branding, electronic shocking, placing of a harmful substance on the body, or similar activity; 2. any type of physical activity, such as sleep deprivation, exposure to the elements, confinement in a small space, calisthenics, or other activity that subjects the student to an unreasonable risk or harm or that adversely affects the mental or physical health or safety of the student; 3. any activity involving consumption of a food, liquid, alcoholic beverage, liquor, drug, or other substance which subjects the student to an unreasonable risk of harm or which adversely effects the mental or physical health or safety of the student; 4. any activity that intimidates or threatens the student with ostracism that subjects the student to extreme mental stress, shame, or humiliation, or that adversely effects the student from entering or remaining registered in an educational institution, or that may reasonably be expected to cause a student to leave the organization or the institution rather than submit to acts described in this subsection; 5. any activity that induces, causes, or requires the student to perform a duty or task which involves a violation of the Penal Code. Sec. 4.52.	Pros • Includes examples of hazing • Notes qualities that are specific to hazing, including when hazing is most likely to occur • Includes psychological harm • Does not limit hazing to initiation or preinitiation Cons • Does not address hazing outside education context • Does not address the consent of the hazed individual(s)

Table 2.1—Continued

Source and Definition	Comments
California Penal Code, Section 245.6	
"Hazing" means any method of initiation or preinitiation into a student organization or student body, whether or not the organization or body is officially recognized by an educational institution, which is likely to cause serious bodily injury to any former, current, or prospective student of any school, community college, college, university, or other educational institution in this state. The term "hazing" does not include customary athletic events or school-sanctioned events.	Cons • Does not include examples of hazing activities • Does not include psychological harm • Limits hazing to initiation or preinitiation, whereas hazing may occur after membership is obtained • Does not address hazing outside education context • Does not address the consent of the hazed individual(s)
North Carolina Criminal Law, Chapter 14	
For the purposes of this section hazing is defined as follows: "to subject another student to physical injury as part of an initiation, or as a prerequisite to membership, into any organized school group, including any society, athletic team, fraternity or sorority, or other similar group."	Cons • Does not include examples of hazing activities • Does not include psychological harm • Does not address the consent of the hazed individual(s) • Limits hazing to initiation or preinitiation, whereas hazing may occur after membership is obtained • Does not address hazing outside education context

Table 2.1—Continued

Source and Definition	Comments
Virginia Crimes and Offenses Law, Title 18.2 "Hazing" means to recklessly or intentionally endanger the health or safety of a student or students or to inflict bodily injury on a student or students in connection with or for the purpose of initiation, admission into or affiliation with or as a condition for continued membership in a club, organization, association, fraternity, sorority, or student body regardless of whether the student or students so endangered or injured participated voluntarily in the relevant activity.	Pros • Addresses the consent of the hazed individual(s) • Does not limit hazing to initiation or preinitiation Cons • Does not include examples of hazing activities • Does not include psychological harm • Does not address hazing outside education context

harm. Most of the definitions do not address the consent of the hazed individual(s), leaving it unclear whether consent may factor into hazing litigation. Finally, as suggested by the previously described research on hazing knowledge, those in these states may have little or no knowledge of the existence or meaning of the definitions.

Additional Definitions of Hazing

Different institutions, organizations, and researchers have also established their own definitions of hazing, with certain of these definitions commonly cited in research and theory on hazing. For example, the Fraternity Insurance Protection Group (FIPG) was developed, in part, to provide policies and practices for fraternities and sororities. This group provides a risk management manual that condemns and defines hazing activities that specifically offers the following definition:

> Any action taken or situation created, intentionally, whether on or off fraternity premises, to produce mental or physical discomfort, embarrassment, harassment, or ridicule. Such activities may include but are not limited to the following: use of alcohol; paddling in any form; creation of excessive fatigue; physical and psychological shocks; quests, treasure hunts, scavenger hunts, road trips or any other such activities carried on outside or inside of the confines of the chapter house; wearing of public apparel which is conspicuous and not normally in good taste; engaging in public stunts and buffoonery; morally degrading or humiliating games and activities; and any other activities which are not consistent with academic achievement, fraternal law, ritual or policy or the regulations and policies of the educational institution or applicable state law. (FIPG, 2008, p. 8)

Because of the purpose of FIPG, this definition is tailored to fraternities and sororities. Importantly, it notes that hazing actions may cause mental or physical discomfort. It also provides example activities that would be considered hazing. However, this definition has several limitations. For example, the definition suggests that acts of hazing are intentional, not recognizing that reckless actions may cause harm, and does not outline the specific points at which hazing is most likely to occur. Despite its limitations, research assessing this definition suggests that it does improve identification of hazing activities (Kittle, 2012).

Researchers also often cite the following NCAA definition of hazing:

> Any act committed against someone joining or becoming a member or maintaining membership in any organization that is humiliating, intimidating or demeaning, or endangers the health and safety of the person. Hazing includes active or passive participation in such acts and occurs regardless of the willingness to participate in the activities! Hazing creates an environment/climate in which dignity and respect are absent. (NCAA, 2007, p. 2)

However, this definition has also been critiqued because it specifies that hazing involves an individual who is joining a group (Crow and Macintosh, 2009); individuals who are hazed can also be those individuals who have already joined the group (e.g., a coach has incorporated them into a team).

Different paramilitary groups, such as police and fire departments, have also developed definitions and policies to address hazing. For example, the Los Angeles Police Department, one of the largest police departments in the United States, defines hazing as "any activity related to initiation which causes, or is likely to cause physical harm, personal degradation, ridicule, criticism, or mental anguish" (Los Angeles Police Department, 2013). However, this definition again has several limitations. Specifically, it does not clarify what constitutes mental anguish, does not list example acts, does not address hazee consent, does not address culpability for authority-sanctioned hazing, and limits hazing to initiation activities.

Finally, in an effort to address limitations in previous hazing definitions and statutes, a "Model Uniform Anti-Hazing Statute" was also developed in the 1990s as an exemplar for those wishing to define and address hazing:

> A person is guilty of hazing in the first degree when, in the course of another person's initiation into or affiliation with any organi-

> zation, he or she intentionally or recklessly engages in conduct or knowingly permits another person under said person's direction or control to engage in conduct which creates a substantial risk of serious physical or mental injury to such other person or a third person, with or without the consent of said other person or third person, and thereby causes such injury. (Lewis, 1991, pp. 145–146)

Assessing the Current DoD Definition of Hazing

On August 28, 1997, DoD issued a memorandum that defined hazing and emphasized that hazing should not be allowed within DoD (see the chapter introduction). This definition notes that hazing can be psychological and need not involve physical contact. It also establishes that the consent of the victim does not eliminate the culpability of hazers. These are attributes of hazing that scholars have suggested are important to note (Pelletier, 2002). In addition, the definition provides examples of hazing activities that may be prevalent in the military context.

However, the scholarly critiques of hazing definitions we described earlier suggest that this definition has some limitations. First, it appears to absolve individuals of responsibility for hazing if the acts have been approved by an authority figure, which may promote perceptions that the armed forces accept some hazing if it has been properly authorized. Second, there may be some subjectivity in assessment of whether an act is "cruel, abusive, humiliating, oppressive, or demeaning," which could further contribute to confusion about when an activity would be considered hazing. Third, although the inclusion of examples has been shown to be helpful (Kittle, 2012), it is not clear how prevalent the acts listed in the DoD definition are within the military today. Instead, drawing on a list of examples that have recently been prosecuted or hazing acts that have been established to be endemic in the armed forces may be more useful. Finally, the definition appears overly broad by stating that hazing is "any activity which is cruel, abusive . . . or harmful." This broad description could encompass other negative behaviors, such as bullying, abusive supervision, or harassment. DoD would certainly like to eliminate all these behaviors. However, to help military members understand and be able to identify hazing specifically, it is important to describe key characteristics of hazing that differentiate it from other types of negative behaviors, such as the focus on initiations, maintenance of group membership, or gaining status within a group. Having a clearer and narrower definition can also help improve tracking of hazing incidents, which is critical to the development of prevention and response efforts.

According to reports to Congress on hazing in the armed forces in July 2013, the Coast Guard and the Department of the Navy, including the U.S. Marine Corps (USMC), use and approve of the above definition. However, the Department of the Army and the Department of the Air Force have recommended changes to this definition. The Department of the Air Force specifically recommended the following definition:

> Hazing is defined as any conduct whereby military member(s) recklessly or intentionally endanger(s) the health or safety of any person, or inflict(s) physical or psychological injury on any person in connection with, or for the purpose of initiation, admission into, affiliation with, or as a condition for continued membership in any military club, organization, association, or career designation if there is no legitimate and officially sanctioned training or operational purpose served by the specific activity. Any person subject to the UCMJ engaging in such conduct may be deemed to have hazed another person regardless of either party's military status, service, or grade, and regardless of whether the person so endangered or injured participated voluntarily in the relevant activity. (U.S. Air Force, 2013)

This definition has several positive attributes. For example, it shows recognition that hazing can involve both physical and psychological injury. It also notes the irrelevance of the consent of participating parties. Further, by identifying acts as specific to initiation, admission, affiliation, and membership, this definition characterizes behaviors specific to hazing, thereby narrowing the breadth of the definition.

However, as with the 1997 DoD definition of hazing, this definition does not clarify that authority-sanctioned hazing is unacceptable. Further, providing examples that have recently been prosecuted or hazing acts that have been established to be endemic in the armed forces may be a useful improvement. A final potential concern is the reference to the UCMJ, a law with which new recruits may have limited familiarity.

Recommendations

As described above, the 1997 DoD definition of hazing includes several key components that scholars have recommended and should continue to be part of any revised hazing definition. These include noting that hazing can be psychological and does not just involve physical contact and that the consent of the victim does not eliminate the culpability of hazers.

However, given our review of the literature and our assessment of current limitations in the 1997 DoD definition, we also recommend the following improvements to DoD's definition for hazing:

- Include qualities that are distinctive to hazing, to distinguish it from other types of abuse and mistreatment. For example, it should be noted that hazing activities are often part of initiations, intended to maintain group membership, or part of a change in status or position within a group.
- Clarify the role of authority figures and the individual's responsibility to address authority-approved hazing. This will help eliminate ambiguity about the culpability of those who engage in authority-sanctioned hazing.
- Consider the use of more-objective terms in describing harm, such as "psychological injury" or "extreme mental stress." These may be used in addition to, or as alternatives to, "humiliating" or "demeaning." The terms used should be clear and specific about the psychological consequences of interest.
- Ensure that the list of examples is based on hazing acts considered to be prevalent within the military today. These could be drawn from recently prosecuted or reported hazing acts or could be based on perceptions of prevalence from service members. These examples can also be used to differentiate hazing from sanctioned

rituals and training exercises. As part any service-specific policies or training, each service may also want to tailor the examples to the acts most common in the particular service.[2]

Conclusion

Confusion about what actions constitute hazing appears to be prevalent across different military and nonmilitary groups. We found the current DoD definition of hazing, established in 1997, to be overly broad and to lack several key components that hazing scholars consider important for providing a clear and understandable definition. Improving the current DoD definition to cover these key components better may help address possible uncertainty about hazing among military personnel and may help improve reporting and tracking of hazing incidents in the future.

It is important to note, though, that clarifying the definition is necessary but may not be enough to address hazing in the armed forces. It will also be necessary to provide the definition to service members and to educate them on its meaning. Chapter Four addresses this and provides additional information on training.

---

2 Since completion of this study, the DoD Hazing Review Team has drafted a revised definition for hazing that incorporates many of these recommendations. The revised definition will be included in new DoD hazing policy.

CHAPTER THREE

The Effects of and Motivations for Hazing

Hazing is often described as involving abuse of potential and new members of a group by a more senior cohort with the goal of bringing them into the group. However, hazing may also include some maltreatment of current members. It is a common practice across different countries, cultures, and societies (Cimino, 2011). Further, hazing or similar ritualistic behaviors, such as religious rituals, have been practiced for centuries (Sosis, 2004). Its widespread, long-term prevalence shows that hazing is not limited to the armed forces, to Western culture, or to recent generations (Cimino and Delton, 2010).

In this chapter, we review theory and research on the motivations for hazing others and submitting to hazing. Broad consideration of the processes that cause people to haze others or to endure being hazed is important for understanding and addressing hazing among the armed forces.

Hazing as a Ritual or Initiation Rite

Research on the motivations for hazing and, in particular, hazing in the military is somewhat limited. However, research and theory on rituals, initiations, and other acts may help increase understanding of why people haze, why those hazed accept it, and why hazing is difficult to stop. Specifically, some of the social and psychological processes that underlie such acts may also contribute to participation in and support for hazing (e.g., Koenig and Bouchard, 2006). Although we draw from theory and research on these other activities to better understand hazing, we are not suggesting that hazing is synonymous, however.

Rituals involve sequences of actions, performed by a group, that have an underspecified or unspecified physical-causal function (Atkinson and Whitehouse, 2011). The distinct purpose of the specific set of group-based actions is vague. Even though the ritual itself may have a stated purpose, the relationship between the actions performed in the ritual and the stated purpose of the ritual is not obvious. Some researchers propose that participation in these opaque actions may contribute to perceptions of group bonding among participants, and the more painful, frightening, or traumatic the actions, the more intense the perceived group bonding (Whitehouse, 1995; Whitehouse, 2012). For example, the uncertainty and confusion the rituals create and subsequent need for certainty and security may contribute to conformity to the group norms and perceived bonding with the group (Dunham, Kidwell, and Wilson, 1986; Sweet, 2004). Examples of opaque, dysphoric rituals that may promote perceptions of group bonding can be found among Melanesian initiations, for instance, which have involved burning, bleeding, piercing, beating, and/or terrifying individuals as part of their transition from novices to full members of the group (see Whitehouse, 1996).

With their opaque purpose, acts of hazing may be considered ritualistic. Although rituals come in various forms, hazing may be closely related to, or similar to, initiation rituals (Atkinson and Whitehouse, 2011; Johnson, 2011). For example, like the rituals of Melanesian initiations, hazing can involve burning, bleeding, piercing, beating, and/or terrifying initiates prior to acceptance into a sports team, band, or fraternity or sorority (Finkel, 2002; Regan, 2013; Simon, 2012; Zezima, 2008).

Initiation rituals can range from tribal customs to coronations but are believed to have certain shared characteristics. Van Gennep (1960) proposed that initiation ceremonies follow a pattern of separation, transition, and incorporation. First, initiates are separated from their previous lives, or from the profane world (e.g., they are separated from their family and previous friends). They then transition to their new lives, or the new world, which may be the world of adults or the world of the sacred. This transition process may involve processes like beatings, mutilations, and intoxication (e.g., rites of terror; Whitehouse, 1996). Finally, initiates are incorporated into their new role, often with a change in appearance, name, or title (e.g., they are accepted as adult members in their small society or as members of a team or group). These stages may be similarly distinguished in military hazing, as recruits are removed from the civilian world and sent through a period of transition. If they are able to survive and endure the transition period, they are incorporated into their new group with a new title.

Unpleasant Training and Hazing

Before continuing, it is also worthwhile to distinguish between acts of hazing and difficult or unpleasant training and tasks. Many groups, including the armed forces, require their members to possess certain skills and abilities. These groups often require members to undergo difficult training or tests to ensure that potential, new, and current members have the skills and abilities needed to perform adequately in the group. This training and the subsequent tests tend to have clear, group-relevant objectives and do not necessarily constitute hazing. In contrast, the activities that hazing requires of members are not related to any particular skills or abilities that are clearly requisite to the group.

Cimino (2011), a researcher who addresses motivations for hazing, made this distinction in describing a hypothetical group called the "Block Holders." Briefly, he noted that the fictitious Block Holders, a group whose only purpose is to carry heavy blocks for several hours each day, may require that potential group members demonstrate they are able to carry heavy blocks for several hours. This would allow assessment of the ability of potential members to perform the group-relevant task of block carrying. Although carrying blocks may be unpleasant, requiring potential members to do so does not necessarily constitute hazing. In contrast, requiring potential members of another group, the "Reading Club," to carry heavy blocks for several hours each day may constitute hazing for that group. In the case of the second group, the objective or purpose of carrying heavy blocks is opaque and not clearly related to group-relevant tasks. Relating this example to the armed forces, Cimino (2011, p. 243) noted that "basic training in the military may be profoundly unpleasant, but much of it is likely understandable in non-hazing terms."

Proposed Effects of Hazing on Hazees

Proponents of hazing argue that acts of hazing or harsh initiation rituals contribute to increased liking of, commitment to, and cohesion with the group. However, evidence for these different effects is mixed, and research and reports demonstrate that hazing can lead to physical and psychological injuries among hazees (Finkel, 2002). Below, we describe these proposed justifications for hazing, including any relevant research findings.

Group Liking and Commitment through Effort Justification

One of the most common justifications for hazing is that it increases group liking and commitment to the group. The well-known theory of cognitive dissonance provides some support for this justification, in that it proposes that one's actions can lead to attitude changes (Stone and Fernandez, 2008). Specifically, individuals whose actions or behaviors are discrepant with their thoughts and attitudes may feel extreme discomfort, or dissonance. To reduce this unpleasant feeling, these individuals may subsequently change their attitudes to correspond with their actions, thereby reducing dissonance. For example, after humans go through trouble or pain to attain something, they may value that object more highly, whether or not it actually warrants that value (Aronson and Mills, 1959). The more trouble or pain they go through, the more they need to justify their efforts to obtain the object and, thus, the more value they place on it. Notably, an "object" may include membership in a group.

Building from this theory, one may expect that participation in hazing would cause attitude-changing dissonance. Hazing could generate feelings within hazees that the group into which they are being initiated is more desirable. To test this, researchers in the 1950s (Aronson and Mills, 1959) subjected volunteers to one of three possible conditions: a severe initiation, a mild initiation, or a control condition.

Participants assigned to the severe initiation condition were required to read extremely embarrassing materials aloud before they could join a group. Those assigned to the mild initiation condition were required to read materials that were somewhat embarrassing, and those assigned to the control condition were not required to read anything. All participants then listened to the same recording, which they were told was an ongoing discussion by the group they had just joined. This discussion was purposefully dull and boring. After listening to the discussion, participants rated the group. Participants in the severe initiation condition expressed more liking for the group than those in the other conditions, which the researchers attributed to being a function of dissonance. Those who had gone through the more-severe initiation felt more dissonance about their actions, so to justify their actions, they adjusted their attitudes about the group. Those in the other conditions presumably felt little or no dissonance and, thus, felt less need to justify their actions and change their attitudes about the group.

Although this early research supported the notion that more-severe initiations create greater liking for a group or increased valuing of group membership, later research has not consistently done so. For example, research that replicated and extended that of Aronson and Mills included a measure of felt embarrassment among participants. This research found that those in the severe initiation condition who felt most embarrassed, and were thus the most affected, rated the group less positively than those who felt less embarrassment (Schopler and Bateson, 1962). Further, other researchers, using real groups formed outside the lab (i.e., sorority members), found that hazing does not facilitate newcomer commitment to a group (Lodewijkx and Syroit, 1997). Instead, that research found that endurance of more-severe acts of hazing was associated with greater negative affect among initiates, and these negative feelings were associated with lower perceptions of group attractiveness, or less liking for the group. This research suggests that, although hazing has been believed to positively affect both group liking and commitment, the actual effect may be negative.

Notably, dissonance is induced when people believe that they have a choice about whether or not to participate in an activity, such as being hazed. If perceived choice in participating in hazing is reduced, feelings of dissonance and the effects of these feelings are likely to be reduced (Harmon-Jones and Harmon-Jones, 2007). Thus, individuals do not feel a need to justify actions that they were forced to perform. The mixed evidence suggests that one should not assume that hazing will inevitably, or very often, induce greater liking for or commitment to the group among those who are hazed.

Group Dependency

More recently, theorists have proposed that hazing may contribute to greater dependency on the group (Keating et al., 2005). Specifically, they noted that feelings of threat may contribute to individual desires to affiliate and bond with others who are similarly threatened and, potentially, to affiliate and bond with the sources, or causes, of threat (Baumeister and Leary, 1995; Dutton and Painter, 1993; Gump and Kulik, 1997). Thus, those who are hazed may depend on the group more, and this may increase their inclinations to affiliate with group members and others who are being hazed.

Some research supports this theory. For example, in a recent series of studies, researchers (Keating et al., 2005) used a survey and two experiments to assess the effects of initiation practices on group-relevant attitudes, skills, and perceptions. In two experiments, participants were exposed to either discomforting initiations (e.g., charades involving acting like a slave or like a dog) or innocuous initiations (e.g., charades involving brushing teeth or reading a newspaper); afterward, multiple measures of social dependency were collected.[1] Results showed that those who were subjected to discomforting, rather than innocuous, initiations conformed to the experimenters' opinions more, tried to stay closer to experimenters, and exhibited greater anxiety when left alone. Discomforting initiations also contributed to greater perceived importance of the group to the participant but not to greater perceived

---

1 To assess conformity, confederates provided unrealistic ratings of the performance of other students on various activities, which was done in the presence of participants. Afterward, the study participants also provided ratings of the students. Then, experimenters compared confederate and participant ratings. To assess closeness, experimenters assessed the extent to which participants pulled a stool closer to a confederate. Participants also completed a series of survey items regarding their mood when left alone.

importance of the participant to the group. Those who endured discomforting initiations thus did not tend to feel that they were important to the group but did tend to feel that the group was important to them. Other studies have also noted a strong social approval goal orientation among those who have been hazed (Waldron and Kowalski, 2009; Waldron, Lynn, and Krane, 2011). Overall, these results tend to support a social dependency explanation for the effects of hazing.

However, other research assessing group cohesion brings a social-dependency explanation for hazing into question. For example, in a study of hazing and team cohesion among college athletes, Van Raalte et al. (2007) found that frequency of exposure to hazing acts was negatively related to perceptions of team cohesion but that positive team-building activities were positively associated with perceptions of team cohesion (but also see Salo and Siebold, 2008). Thus, based on available evidence, hazing may increase temporary dependency on the group, but it is not yet clear how hazing influences other group-relevant perceptions, including perceptions of group unity and solidarity. Further, the association between perceptions of group unity and dependency also remains unclear.

Proposed Factors Contributing to Support for Hazing Among Hazers

Additional theories about hazing focus primarily on why hazees begin or continue to endure hazing and why hazers choose to participate in these acts. These theories thus emphasize the factors that motivate hazing, rather than the potential effects of enduring acts of hazing. We describe several of these theories and related research below.

Display of Commitment to the Group

Research suggests that ritualistic acts, such as hazing, may be popular and pervasive because they allow participants to display, or signal, their commitment to a group. By displaying more group commitment, participants may receive more group rewards. Thus, participation in highly unpleasant, painful, or embarrassing actions, such as those involved in hazing, serves to demonstrate greater participant commitment to the group. In describing this theoretical notion, Sosis, Kress, and Boster (2007, p. 235) stated that "individuals pay the costs of ritual performance, but by doing so they demonstrate their commitment and loyalty to the group and can thus achieve a net benefit from successful collective action." Similarly, Henrich (2009, p. 245) noted that "[p]articipation in costly rituals is associated with prosocial ingroup behavior, because costly rituals transmit commitment to group-beneficial beliefs/goals to participants." In support of this, various studies describe and support the notion that costly group acts communicate greater group commitment and engender greater trust and subsequent rewards for participants (Henrich, 2009; Levine and Moreland, 1994; Sosis, Kress, and Boster, 2007; Sosis and Ruffle, 2003). By participating in hazing, those who are being hazed may desire to enhance their credibility and show deeper group commitment, thereby promoting the likelihood of group rewards.

Notably, in the armed forces, multiple sanctioned requirements should already be sufficiently challenging to address the purposes of displaying group commitment and enhancing credibility. However, in a military environment in which there is strong dependence on fellow team members, particularly in combat situations, hazing activities may be seen as an extra step in ensuring that all individuals are fully committed to the group and can be trusted.

Prevention of Free Riders in the Group

Related to theory on individuals signaling their commitment to the group, members may support acts of hazing performed by and on others because this permits identification and removal of free riders—those who take the benefits of group membership without paying the costs for them. Groups that offer members greater benefits (e.g., more protection, more resources) and require greater cooperation from group members may be at greater risk of being exposed to and suffering from free riders. Thus, members of these groups may have more negative responses to untested newcomers and may be more likely to utilize actions, such hazing, to ensure members remain committed and to expel free riders (Cimino and Delton, 2010; Sosis, Kress, and Boster, 2007).

Supporting this theory, Cimino and Delton (2010) found that new members of a group are viewed more negatively than veteran members. Specifically, the researchers found that new members were perceived as less trustworthy, less competent, less likeable, and less worthy of group benefits than those with longer tenure. Because of such negative perceptions, veteran group members may desire to test newcomer commitment, and as noted above, this may be particularly likely in highly cooperative and rewarding groups. In additional research supporting this, Cimino (2011) found that individuals desired more-severe hazing in more strongly cooperative groups and were more likely to promote hazing in groups that offered immediate, rather than nonimmediate (i.e., nonautomatic), benefits to newcomers. Further, individuals who contributed more to a group were supportive of more-severe hazing. Overall, this research provides evidence that hazing is often used as a means of preventing free riding. That is, it allows groups to expel or keep out members who will take advantage of group benefits without contributing to group functioning or resources.

Again, sanctioned procedures and requirements are already in place to address potential free riders in the military. However, with groups requiring high levels of cooperation and having the potential for high risks and rewards, hazing may be seen as an effective method of eliminating potential free riders.

Maintenance of Group Structure

Another potential reason for group members to support hazing is that it may serve to maintain a certain organization of, or power structure within, the group. Acts of hazing may be more likely to occur in groups with formal hierarchical structures than in more egalitarian groups because hazing may serve to promote the power of veterans and leaders within the group over newer or subordinate group members (Keating et al., 2005). For example, scholars have noted that more veteran or more powerful group members may use acts of hazing to assert their dominance over others and to maintain their positions of power within the group (e.g., Cimino, 2011). Thus, hazing may be used to communicate the group's structure to new members and to maintain the group hierarchy among current members.

Research assessing the association between initiations, or hazing, and power differentials provides mixed support for a theory of hazing as a technique used to promote structure, however. For example, Keating et al. (2005) found that harsher treatment of initiates seemed to empower those individuals, thereby weakening their cognition regarding group structure and power of group members. In contrast, Cimino (2011) found greater support for hazing of new members by more veteran members, suggesting some support for this theory. Overall, however, because limited research is available on hazing for maintenance of group structure, it is not yet clear whether hazing serves this theorized purpose. Notably, the armed forces already have a clear group structure, maintained through established responsibilities, displays of rank on uniforms, and punishments. Therefore, even if hazing can maintain a certain group structure, the current accepted policies and procedures of the armed forces make hazing unnecessary.

A Taxonomy of Hazing in the Military

To help better conceptualize hazing in the military, we present a basic taxonomy of military hazing. This taxonomy draws from existing research on hazing and group dynamics discussed above to show three major types of hazing, illustrated through recent examples of hazing from the U.S. military. A clearer conception of what hazing looks like, and a basis for interpreting the motivations and dynamics of military hazing, may assist the development of more-targeted prevention and response efforts.

Our review of the literature led us to group theories of hazing into three higher-order types, as shown in Table 3.1. Although there is certainly overlap among these types, this taxonomy is meant to capture salient distinctions in the quality and ends of different types of hazing. For example, hazing in the form of initiation rituals is distinct from other forms in its particular emphasis on ceremony and ritual, regardless of rank. Newcomer testing is distinct in that the participants' goal

Table 3.1
Hazing Taxonomy

Hazing Type	Description
Initiation ritual	Ceremonies and rituals that mark entry or transition
Newcomer testing	Tests intended to prove new members' commitment or solidarity and to screen out those free riding to obtain the benefits of group membership
Maintenance of group structure	Exercise of dominance by more powerful members over weaker members to maintain existing power arrangements and enforce group norms

is to protect their institution by weeding out the unworthy. Hazing to maintain the group structure is distinct in its use of aggression to maintain existing power arrangements.

Finer divisions in hazing theories and types have been combined to create more useful, internally connected categories for classifying and interpreting types of hazing incidents. For example, under the "newcomer testing" category, we grouped together three theories of hazing that are closely related in that they focus on how intergenerational coalitions frame and treat new members. In grouping related theories into a more manageable taxonomy of types, we still retain precision—for example, capturing the qualitative difference between the aggressive character of "maintenance of group structure" hazing and the institutional tradition character of "initiation ritual" hazing.

Not all the activities that could fall into this taxonomy constitute hazing. For example, there are legitimate, sanctioned initiation rituals in the U.S. military that do not constitute hazing, alongside unsanctioned, informal traditions of initiation that do constitute hazing. Similarly, the U.S. military has institutional screening and evaluation practices that test newcomers, prevent free riding, etc. This hazing taxonomy helps show that hazing is not defined by the activities or goals but by characteristics: coercive, abusive, illegitimate versions of sanctioned practices.

The following sections present examples of hazing in the U.S. military and are meant to illustrate each of these types of hazing. We have chosen examples that amply illustrate the characteristics of the particular types of hazing and that have received enough media attention that they may be familiar to readers.

Initiation Rituals

Initiation rituals symbolically recognize when someone has undergone a culturally meaningful change, as members of a group leave behind their old lives and identities and take up new ones (Van Gennep, 1960). Military membership is marked by initiation rituals. For example, in the USMC's "Crucible" initiation rite, new enlisted Marines face a physically and mentally grueling final test before being recognized formally as a member (Garamone, no date). The culminating ceremony for the three-day ritual is a symbolic crossing over from outsider status as recruits: At dawn on the last day of the Crucible, the exhausted recruits cross a bridge and march back to their barracks area; after raising the colors, prayer, and a ceremonial speech, drill instructors hand recruits their service insignia (the eagle, globe, and anchor) and refer to them as "Marines" for the first time. When the recruits finish the Crucible, "a significant transformation takes place" (Garamone, no date), and thereafter they enjoy membership status as Marines. The other services, along with many military subcultures organized around job or mission specialties, each have their version of similar sanctioned initiation rituals. However, unsanctioned initiation rituals also occur, which would constitute hazing. We discuss examples of these below.

Blood Wings

A fairly well-known example of initiation ritual hazing is *blood pinning*: pinning insignia on without protective backing, so that fist blows drive the insignia's metal pins into the hazed member's flesh. Blood pinning can be for rank insignia when a member is promoted or for special insignia, such as jump wings or scuba bubbles. In 1997, videotape of USMC reconnaissance "Gold Wing" ceremonies surfaced (McIntyre, 1997). In the 1991 videos, junior recon Marines who had qualified for paratrooper jump wings were blood pinned: lined up against a wall to have their wings driven into their chests by the rest of the unit (approximately 30 other Marines). The video shows a particularly brutal variant of a blood pinning ceremony. In addition to single or double-fist blows to drive the wings in, many of the hazers start off by using their thumbs to twist and gouge the victims' chests, until many of the victims are screaming in pain, their T-shirts soaked with blood.

News coverage of the story, including a Dateline NBC broadcast that showed graphic footage of the hazing, led to public outcry and repudiation from senior service and DoD officials (Kozaryn, 1997). While these officials reiterated a zero-tolerance policy for hazing, the episode serves to point to the durability of hazing rituals.

Prop and Cherry Blasts

While the blood wings episode may be familiar, another rich and well-documented example illustrates the range of initiation rituals in hazing. In U.S. Army paratroop divisions, the rituals known as "prop blasts" and "cherry blasts," for new officer and enlisted members, respectively, show both the ceremonial and abusive aspects of initiation ritual hazing. These rituals date back to the 1940s (Melchior, 1991) but have evolved over the years. Prop blasts were forbidden for four years after 1967, then were reinstated in a milder form.

In 1982, a cherry blast left a soldier seriously injured and resulted in a court martial that turned public scrutiny on the practice within the 82nd Airborne Division (Daniels, 1992).[2] Robert Daniels, a University of North Carolina anthropologist, was called in by defense counsel to provide context for blasts, allowing Daniels access to document the practices in detail.

At the time of the investigation, prop blasts were division-sanctioned events, involving the division's commanding general and staff. While prop blasts did not involve explicit coercion, and officers were often eager to participate and thereby legitimize their membership, strong social pressure and career prospects made these events obligatory. Like many initial rituals, they followed a three-stage rebirthing formula: *separation* (from the old world) through ritual public humiliation; *transition* (between worlds) through a kind of hand-to-hand wrestling event called "the Bear Pit"; and *reincorporation* (into the new

---

[2] The 1982 investigation documented prop and cherry blasts at the time in great detail. We are not aware of any recent documented cases.

world) with a mock jump, baptism (through drinking noxious liquids), and ritual welcoming into the division as a card-carrying member (Daniels, 1992).

Cherry blasts were more informal, more directly coercive, and more violent. Unlike prop blasts, which were uniformly applied to all officers and consistent in practice, cherry blasts in the 82nd Airborne were selective in application, reflected racial tensions at the time (racially segregated, e.g., same-race hazing along black and white lines), were male only, and varied in content and intensity (Daniels, 1992). Common elements in a cherry blast included veteran troopers overpowering newcomers, stripping them naked, physically assaulting (beating and/or biting) them, tying them up in their sleeping bags, and then suspending them out second-story windows (Daniels, 1992). In some cases, the victim was then dropped out the window and sometimes incurred serious injuries; some victims were also held down in a shower and painted with noxious substances.

Because cherry blasts were more variable in who was targeted and in the severity of the hazing and because more-severe cases were marked by violence and physical coercion, cherry blasts may seem on the surface to more closely match common ideas about hazing. Cherry blasts also partake of the character of hazing focused on maintaining the group structure (described in detail below), in addition to initiation rituals. However, the more-genteel prop blasts for officers can also be seen as a type of hazing: Even though the prop blasts were sanctioned locally by the command and were positioned discursively as "good fun" (Daniels, 1992), they were aimed at newcomers, were implicitly socially coercive, and involved humiliation.

The difference in variability between prop and cherry blasts may point to ceremony as a constraint within ritual initiation hazing practices. Prop blasts were less severe than cherry blasts, and the range of severity of the cherry blasts was wide, with a relatively high ceiling (hence the injuries that eventually led to an investigation). These differences in severity, and the variability in severity, may reflect culture and class divisions between officer and enlisted castes (Daniels, 1992). But the difference in variability may also reflect the relative levels of ceremony. Prop blasts were highly ceremonial and public long-standing traditions and thus had much less room for variability. Cherry blasts, as private and ad hoc events, had much more room for variation.

Newcomer Testing

Theories of newcomer testing argue that groups frame and treat newcomers in structured ways that serve the group's end. While there are important distinctions between these theories, they are connected in that, in some way, they protect the group from perceived risks in admitting newcomers:

- *Group commitment and liking* theories argue that the hazed justify their effort in enduring hazing through greater commitment to the group (Aronson and Mills, 1959).
- *Group dependency* theories argue that hazing may produce a Stockholm Syndrome–like affiliation with the group (Keating et al., 2005).
- *Commitment display* theories position hazing as a way in which existing members test newcomers before trusting them—newcomers must demonstrate their loyalty and commitment before being awarded meaningful membership (Henrich, 2009; Levine and Moreland, 1994; Sosis, Kress, and Boster, 2007; Sosis and Ruffle, 2003).
- *Free riding* theories explain hazing as a costly entry fee to prevent new members from gaining automatic membership benefits (Cimino and Delton, 2010; Cimino, 2011).

The U.S. military has built-in membership tests that make local and unsanctioned testing redundant, and these legitimate tests scale with the stakes for membership. For example, all military members undergo sanctioned, rigorous screening and testing during recruitment and initial training; Special Operations units have additional sanctioned screening and testing (e.g. the Army Special Forces Qualification Course, U.S. Marine Corps Forces Special Operations Command Assessment and Selection) that matches the higher selectivity of such units.

Hazing rituals at U.S. service academies are good examples of unsanctioned newcomer testing, with older members (seniors) directing complex systems to test newcomers (plebes). Although hazing is banned at all U.S. service academies, it has persisted as a problem at these institutions precisely because cadets and midshipmen value their group and feel it is "their responsibility to screen new members and shape those that [do] not fit the mold of their particular institution" (Manzanedo, 2013, p. 15). In both the early 1900s and 1990s, public scandals over hazing at both the U.S. Military Academy at West Point and the U.S. Naval Academy spurred major efforts to reform fourth-class (plebe) systems and prevent hazing, yet hazing has continued as a long-standing problem at both schools (Groah, 2005).

Hazing rituals at the service academies differ in specifics but have in common that older members create a separate testing and commitment system alongside the already demanding organic testing of being a cadet or midshipman. In this version of newcomer testing, instead of seeing the fourth-class system as a means of developing junior members, it is framed as a way to weed out low performers and unfit candidates (Groah, 2005), and a means to create in-group solidarity (Dornbusch, 1955). This service academy culture of newcomer testing has proved durable. For example, the Naval Academy responded to a 1992 GAO report on hazing at the service academies with large-scale reform measures meant to prevent hazing. The GAO report came in the wake of some incidents publicized in the media.[3] Despite these reforms, follow-up research in 2005 found that 92 percent of midshipmen in the 2005–2009 cohorts had been hazed at least once, with a wide variety in the types of hazing (Groah, 2005, p. 57). Commonly reported hazing activities included verbal abuse, extended bracing (holding an exaggerated position of attention), memorizing and reciting trivia, having their rooms or uniforms trashed, and being hosed

[3] Readers may recall an example in which midshipman Gwen Dreyer was forcibly handcuffed to a urinal and taunted by male midshipmen who mimed urinating at her, while other male midshipmen forcibly kept other female midshipmen out of the bathroom (Glionna, 1990).

down and/or pelted with water balloons.[4] Less commonly reported hazing activities included public humiliation (including being smeared with food or shaving cream), forced exercise, personal servitude to seniors, and missing meals to recite trivia. Rarely reported hazing activities included physical intimidation, being tied up or restrained, forced alcohol consumption, simulating sex, and head-dunking in toilets.

The hazing practices listed in the above paragraph cover a wide range. At one end are acts that fit popular notions of hazing, such as humiliation and smearing with food. At the other end are acts that are not intrinsically demeaning or abusive—for example, forced exercise and memorizing and reciting trivia are commonplace at service recruit training. However, they all form an illegitimate, unsanctioned set of tests applied unfairly to newcomers and thus could be considered hazing. Newcomer testing as reported at the service academies seems to present a particular challenge because of the deeply held cultural belief of many members that it is their responsibility to guard the institution by weeding out low performers, in direct tension with the institution's explicit policy. We note, however, that hazing activity, at least at the Naval Academy, appears to have declined significantly in the intervening 13 years (Groah, 2005).

Maintenance of Group Structure

Another set of theories argues that hazing is a means of social control, asserting and supporting existing group structures and power arrangements (Cimino, 2011; Waldron and Kowalski, 2009). From this perspective, hazing can be understood as the imposition of dominance "that requires new members to show subservience to old members" (Nuwer, 2001). While the U.S. military structure is characterized by hierarchical power arrangements along lines of seniority, this type of hazing by older members of new members is distinct in its abusive character and in that it does not reflect normal relations between members.

An egregious example of this type of hazing comes from a dog-handler incident in the Military Working Dog Unit, Bahrain Weapons

---

4 "Common" activities were reported by 50 percent or more of the cohort, "less common" by more than 25 percent, and "rarely reported" acts by 25 percent.

of Mass Destruction Detachment. The U.S. Navy command investigation found a pattern of abuse and misconduct on the part of the senior chief petty officer of the detachment (U.S. Navy, 2007; Liewer, 2009). Newcomers were systematically hazed, with activities that included being locked into feces-filled dog kennels, being forcibly hog-tied, being subjected to public humiliation (including having to "bark like a b---h" and "quack like a duck" while chewing a mouthful of dog treats), and doing pushups on hot pavement to blister hands, among other activities (U.S. Navy, 2007, p. 4).[5] There was also a strong component of sexual harassment. Female newcomers and male newcomers suspected of being homosexual were tied up with same-sex partners and forced to simulate sex acts while being sniffed by dogs, under the guise of training. While all new members of the unit were dominated, female and suspected gay members may have been perceived as particularly vulnerable or as being threats because of their difference from an implicit male, heterosexual norm (Winslow, 1999).

When the hazing practices of this unit became public, they received national attention in the media, bringing disrepute on the entire service. One noncommissioned officer who had been singled out for the most severe and continuous hazing (for suspicion of being homosexual), experienced such great distress over his treatment that, even after admission into the Naval Academy prep school, he resigned from the service (Rocha, 2009). The second-most-senior noncommissioned officer in the unit was charged for failing to stop the hazing and, while on legal hold in Bahrain, killed herself in her personal quarters (Liewer, 2009; Rocha, 2009).

In addition to the above example, part of maintaining the group structure is through monitoring and enforcement of group norms and values. This can provide critical incentives for members to contribute to the good of the group, particularly in smaller groups (Levine and Modica, 2014), such as military units. Peer monitoring and discipline are critical to the development of cohesion among military members and can be done in appropriate and legitimate ways. For example, in

[5] The list of hazing activities reported in the investigation is much lengthier—here we list only a few examples that communicate the nature of the hazing.

the socialization of new U.S. Marines, public displays of approval and disapproval provide powerful incentives for members to place the good of the group above their own individual benefit (Marcellino, 2013). However, discipline and the policing of behavior boundaries for group members can also be done in illicit, illegitimate ways that are abusive and constitute hazing (Stoudt, 2006). In the context of the armed forces, this can lead to complex situations in which group members seek a valid end (cohesion and mutual helping behavior) but do so in abusive ways.

On April 3, 2011, USMC Lance Corporal Harry Lew committed suicide in Helmand Province, Afghanistan, after an extended bout of what was considered hazing from others in his squad. The command investigation into Lew's suicide found this to be the culmination of intense conflict in the squad over Lew's continued endangerment of his fellow marines through his misconduct (U.S. Marine Corps, 2011; Ni, 2011). On March 23, 2011, Lew's first day with his new squad, the squad was involved in a firefight with enemy forces; later that night, Lew fell asleep on watch while the unit was in the field in combat operations. A few days later, while on an ambush patrol, Lew again fell asleep on watch, threatening the safety and lives of his fellow Marines. On April 2, Lew yet again was caught asleep on watch, this time by senior leaders from the battalion and regimental command. All the incidents of sleeping on watch took place when enemy attack was imminent, a serious legal offense in the U.S. military, punishable in the extreme by a sentence of death (10 USC 47). Lew's unit was concerned that he was a threat to their lives, and after peer counseling failed, his chain of command informed him he would be subject to nonjudicial punishment for his continued offenses.

On April 3, Lew once again fell asleep on post; at this time, the unit squad leader (a sergeant) broadcast on the radio that "peers should correct peers," essentially green-lighting hazing in response to Lew's misconduct (U.S. Marine Corps, 2011, p. 5). Two lance corporal peers of Lew's then forced Lew to walk rounds in full gear while carrying a sandbag (symbolic of his deadweight to the squad), forced him to exercise to exhaustion in full gear, verbally and physically abused him (including punches and kicks during exercise), poured the sandbag out on his face when he stopped exercising, and forced him to dig a new fighting hole.[6] At the end of this multihour session, at 3:43 a.m. on April 3, Lew put the barrel of his automatic weapon in his mouth and pulled the trigger, killing himself.

It is important to note though that there is some question as to whether this incident constituted hazing or bullying in terms of whether the goal was to bring Lew into the group or to exclude him and get him to drop out. Assuming the actions were designed to reinforce Lew's commitment to the group structure and norms, the incident may serve as an example of hazing and shows the worst possible negative outcome.

Conclusion

Supporters of hazing propose that it has many positive benefits, claiming that it promotes friendships and leads to group bonding (e.g., the narratives in Waldron, Lynn, and Krane, 2011). However, research on the effects of hazing is mixed and generally seems to suggest that hazing does not contribute to greater liking for the group or greater perceptions of group cohesion among those who are hazed. However, it may contribute to greater feelings of social dependency on the group among those who are hazed.

In terms of motivations for hazing, theory and research suggest that individuals endure hazing to signal their commitment to group members and, thus, to receive the benefits of group membership. In addition, hazers may use hazing to eliminate free riders and maintain power differentials within the group. This chapter has applied these motivations to examples of hazing in the military to develop an initial taxonomy of types of military hazing. Alongside a more-extended theoretical discussion of hazing theories and definition, this taxonomy may be useful in conceptualizing hazing in the U.S. military. We selected a wide range of examples that cover not only a variety of hazing prac-

---

6 A deliberate fighting hole is a chest-deep hole with a protective berm, and digging one is physically exhausting.

tices but also the diverse locations and conditions under which hazing can occur. A richer understanding through a taxonomy of hazing in the U.S. military, and insight into member goals, may inform policy responses in ways that fit the particulars and context of U.S. military culture. The goal is plausible solutions that fit the realities of contemporary hazing in the military.

Broad consideration of the processes that cause people to haze others or to endure being hazed may assist in better understanding and addressing hazing among the armed forces. For example, as a very hierarchical organization in which individuals operate as highly cooperative teams, often in high-risk environments, the military may be particularly predisposed for hazing incidents to occur and become embedded in the culture. Therefore, knowing the types of situations in which hazing may be most likely to occur and potential attitudes toward such activities can help the services better target prevention activities. Further, it is important to note that the armed forces already have a series of sanctioned actions, policies, and procedures that demonstrate group commitment and maintain hierarchical group structure. Thus, engaging in hazing in the armed forces adds no value.

CHAPTER FOUR

Preventing and Responding to Hazing in the Armed Forces

Hazing can cause severe psychological or physical harm (Finkel, 2002). Aware of this, multiple sources have identified potential avenues for preventing and responding to hazing within an organization, school, or community (Allan and Madden, 2008; Lipkins, 2006; Nuwer, 2001; Waldron, 2012). These proposed avenues often build from observations regarding hazing attitudes and behaviors and also incorporate previous theory and research on interventions for addressing violence, discrimination, sexual assault, and other negative behaviors. However, comprehensive antihazing efforts have not been systematically evaluated. Thus, the extent to which the proposed avenues are associated with hazing reduction remains unclear.

This chapter synthesizes information on practices for hazing prevention and response and provides an assessment of the current state of antihazing training in the armed forces. We draw from information obtained from the literature on hazing prevention, antihazing training, and related topics (e.g., bullying prevention, violence prevention, and sexual assault prevention), as well as on information from semistructured interviews with subject-matter experts on the topics of hazing and hazing prevention (see Appendix A for more details on our methodology). We also draw from our previously presented information on definitions of hazing and consider the hazing definitions that the services provide during training. Building from this information, we conclude with a list of several broad areas that should be addressed within the armed forces' antihazing prevention and response efforts.

Potential Levels of Antihazing Efforts

During interviews, subject-matter experts in hazing prevention noted that there are different levels of change or prevention that must be considered when implementing a program of prevention or intervention.[1] These can include personal, interpersonal, group, intergroup, organizational, and community levels of change (Ferdman and Brody, 1996). For example, a hazing program aimed at implementing change at the individual level may address the knowledge, attitudes, and behaviors of individual military service members. By contrast, a program aimed at change at the organizational or institutional level may focus on policies and practices that the service or DoD promotes. The specific components and qualities of an antihazing effort address certain levels of change, and what level specific components are most likely to influence should be considered. As a more detailed example, Appendix B provides a thorough description of comprehensive hazing reform that took place at FAMU following the hazing-related death of a drum major. The description addresses different potential aspects of antihazing efforts described below.

Organization-Level Efforts

Individuals operate within systems, so researchers propose taking the system and context into account in most program designs. Efforts that focus solely on addressing an undesired behavior or set of behaviors at the individual level have been called misguided and found to be ineffective (Bond and Hauf, 2007; Hage et al., 2007). Specifically, considering only the proximal factors that influence a person may place excessive blame on that person and may not sufficiently account for the influence of the organization and broader social context in which that person acts. Response and prevention efforts that include a systemwide approach, such as by incorporating organizational rules and sanctions and leader or supervisor training, may be more effective at reducing

---

1 Interview with Caroline Keating, March 12, 2014; Interview with Jennifer Waldron, March 11, 2014.

negative behaviors within the institution or organization (Vreeman and Carroll, 2007).

Applying these general ideas about levels of change to the context of hazing, Linda Langford (2008), an expert on hazing and violence prevention, proposed a comprehensive framework for hazing prevention. To address the group- and organizational-level elements that may contribute to hazing practices, she suggested implementing antihazing policies, enforcing them, and having higher-level leaders at the organizational level oversee the groups.

Supporting this proposition of organization-level antihazing efforts, other researchers have noted that hazing often occurs in organizational contexts in which there is "slothful supervision" (Edelman, 2005, p. 314). For example, individuals in positions of authority may know about the hazing but take no action to address it.[2] This inaction can communicate to hazers and hazees that the practice is accepted by leadership and the organization, thereby promoting its continuation. This suggests that organizational policies and programs that encourage supervision should be considered.

Organization-Level Punishment

To promote change at the organizational level, researchers suggest that efforts involve both elements that are primarily focused on punishment, which may later contribute to prevention among those who see or experience the punishment, and elements that promote prevention, with less emphasis on punishment (Dixon, 2001). Organization-level punishment may involve increased accountability of the organization, of groups within the organization, and of authorities within the group (Edelman, 2005). During interviews, subject-matter experts provided several comments on and recommendations for organization-level punishment. Proposed avenues for increasing accountability that were mentioned during interviews include requiring those in positions of authority to report hazing or suspected hazing and implementing severe sanctions against authority figures who do not do so.[3] To pro-

---

2 Interview with Mary Madden, March 4, 2014.

3 Interview with R. Brian Crow, March 6, 2014.

mote their awareness of hazing and ability to identify its occurrence, these authority figures should be trained on how to detect hazing.[4] Additional recommended forms of organization-level hazing punishment efforts include a well-publicized hazing policy that outlines the consequences for participating in hazing and organizational policies that require hazing be dealt with swiftly and visibly.[5]

In the armed forces, the broader social context may include the service or a smaller unit within the service. An antihazing effort within the armed forces that aligns with recommendations for organization-level punishment should therefore include careful consideration of DoD and service antihazing policies to ensure that that they include clear definitions and well-defined consequences. In addition, these efforts may also include strong oversight of certain unit activities, swift and visible action against hazers and units that haze, and severe consequences for unit leaders who permit hazing.

Organization-Level Prevention

Organization-level policies and practices that focus primarily on prevention emphasize communication and tracking. For example, proposed strategies include clear reporting methods that those who might report hazing incidents perceive as confidential or anonymous and thus safe.[6] As with reporting of sexual assault incidents, many individuals may be afraid to come forward out of fear of repercussions from peers or even leadership. This inhibits the ability to help those who may need it following an incident or the ability to respond effectively and prevent future incidents. Organizational-level prevention strategies also include maintaining accurate and widely available records of hazing. These records of hazing would inform individuals considering membership within a group of its recent history of hazing and improve the ability of the larger organization to supervise the group (Nicoletti, Spencer-Thomas, and Bollinger, 2001). Another prevention-focused strategy

---

4 Interview with Susan Lipkins, March 5, 2014.

5 Hoover, 1999, and interviews with Charles Hall, March 6, 2014, and Judy Van Raalte, March 5, 2014.

6 Interview with Judy Van Raalte, March 5, 2014.

includes assignment of an individual or group both to oversee antihazing efforts and to hold responsible for ensuring their proper implementation (e.g., Kalev, Kelly, and Dobbin, 2006).

In the armed forces, initial steps have been taken to address hazing prevention at the organizational level. For example, the U.S. Navy has created an office that tracks hazing and oversees antihazing efforts. Similar efforts may be worthwhile to consider across the armed forces. Further, providing service members with options for reporting hazing beyond just the ability to report to their chain of command may result in a greater number of hazing incidents being addressed and stopped and the ability to prevent future incidents. For example, these may include a confidential or anonymous hotline or online reporting mechanism. Finally, the accuracy of the hazing records the armed forces currently maintain is problematic. Maintenance of accurate records of hazing allegations may assist prevention by promoting greater oversight of units with higher numbers of substantiated allegations. Chapter Five provides additional analysis and description of reporting and recordkeeping in the armed forces.

Individual-Level Efforts

Individual-level antihazing efforts focus on the provision of antihazing education courses. Although many antihazing education workshops and courses exist, they have not been systematically evaluated, so their utility in reducing or preventing hazing remains unknown. However, theory and research from other areas can inform the design of antihazing education.

Generally, educational efforts involving aspects of prevention, intervention, or social change emphasize three primary components: knowledge, attitudes and perceptions, and behaviors and skills (Driscoll, 2000; Ferdman and Brody, 1996). This suggests that an antihazing training educational program should address each of these elements.[7] Further, building from a learning model of behavior, it may be worthwhile to approach these three components sequentially (Kirkpatrick, 1996; Valente, Paredes, and Poppe, 1998). For example,

---

[7] Interview with Judy Van Raalte, March 5, 2014.

many participants may have little or no knowledge of the characteristics of hazing or policies on hazing, so addressing comprehension of these elements may be a necessary first step.

Knowledge

An educational effort that emphasizes increasing knowledge tends to focus on providing facts and information (Ferdman and Brody, 1996). This may include providing details about definitions, practices, and policies within an organization.[8] The objective of this education is not to address attitudes or behaviors but rather to ensure that participants understand basic facts, concepts, and organizational rules. Later training may then build from participant knowledge of these concepts. Antihazing training that promotes knowledge may include a definition and description of hazing, detailing several examples to which participants may be exposed. In addition, this knowledge-focused antihazing training may include a clear and concise description of the policy on hazing; a thorough description of the legal, physical, and psychological consequences of hazing; and an explanation of the available reporting avenues and of the processes that occur during and after reporting. Specific to the armed forces, this information should also include examples and information that help individuals differentiate hazing from sanctioned activities, including military training activities or extra military instruction (i.e., assigning extra tasks to correct behavioral or performance issues).

Attitudes and Perceptions

The second suggested element to address in antihazing training is attitudes and perceptions. An attitude can be conceptualized as an evaluative judgment that combines the cognitive and affective responses that a person holds on a particular topic (Prislin and Crano, 2008). An attitude toward hazing is one's evaluation of hazing and involves a positive or negative assessment of such acts or rites. Antihazing training addressing attitudes may discuss misperceptions about the positive attributes of hazing, such as incorrect beliefs that hazing inevitably increases cohesion (see Van Raalte et al., 2007). To avoid participant

---

8 Interview with R. Brian Crow, March 6, 2014.

defensiveness, this must be done carefully and with consideration of the characteristics of participants' histories with and beliefs about hazing. For example, participants may have previously participated in hazing activities in high school (Allan and Madden, 2008) and may feel a defensive need to justify their previous participation in these activities.

Perceptions about hazing can include perceived norms and perceived behavioral control. Both attitudes and perceptions can influence behavioral inclinations regarding hazing (Ajzen, 1991; Richardson, Wang, and Hall, 2012). Social norms are common, shared behaviors within a society or group (Schultz, Tabanico, and Rendon, 2008). Antihazing training that addresses hazing norms may address perceptions about how prevalent hazing is within the armed forces and certain units (i.e., descriptive norms) and perceptions about the level of support for hazing (i.e., injunctive norms). Perceptions of behavioral control involve judgments about one's confidence in and ability to perform an action. Antihazing training addressing perceived behavioral control may invoke feelings of personal responsibility and promote confidence in addressing hazing. As several of the subject-matter experts we interviewed noted, this topic may be especially worthwhile in promoting action among bystanders who see or know about hazing but may not feel confident in or responsible for addressing hazing.[9]

Different training efforts that have been designed to address attitudes and perceptions on a particular topic are often ill-conceived and have the potential to contribute to participant backlash (Bingham and Scherer, 2001; Pendry, Driscoll, and Field, 2007). For example, simply informing people that their past participation in and current perceptions about hazing are wrong may lead participants to feel threatened, and they may become defensive. Those providing antihazing training should therefore first understand what participant's attitudes are about hazing and then use methods that address these attitudes in ways that are unlikely to prompt anger, defensiveness, and backlash, such as those in the literature on social psychology. In the military context, this may be particularly important, given that many hazing activities have been

---

[9] Interviews with Mary Madden, March 4, 2014, and Jennifer Waldron, March 11, 2014.

passed down over generations and, as discussed in Chapter Three, may be perceived to hold a valuable purpose given the military context.

Skills and Behaviors

Systematic evaluations of the influence of training on behaviors are limited across multiple research areas (e.g., Kulik and Roberson, 2008). Hazing training that addresses skills and behaviors would focus on identifying and developing the skills needed to combat hazing. For example, as part of their national study on hazing among college students, Allan and Madden (2008) recommended designing efforts that foster critical thinking skills that may promote ethical decisionmaking when facing hazing. This may help prevent individuals from engaging in hazing others but may also help promote bystander intervention in hazing incidents. Allan and Madden (2008) also recommend that efforts focus on developing leadership skills for preventing and intervening in hazing and on developing strategies for activities that promote group unity without involving hazing. This may be especially important in the military context; military leaders should have the skills and behavioral inclinations to address hazing within their units. Skill- or behavior-focused antihazing training would thus inform individuals how they can help reduce hazing and, more specifically, what actions they can take in response to hazing (e.g., how to report, provide swift discipline, and foster alternative group activities).

Active Versus Passive Learning

Many training efforts involve PowerPoint presentations that are given by a trainer who encourages little or no discussion with participants. This lecture-based format is particularly common when trainers must cover a large amount of material in a short time. These kinds of lecture-based training efforts are likely to promote passive learning, such that participants are expected to absorb and memorize the material but are not encouraged to actively engage with it. Although passive learning may increase knowledge on a topic, training methods that encourage discussion, active engagement with the materials, and critical thinking instill more knowledge and promote longer retention (Burke and Hutchins, 2007; Deslauriers, Schelew, and Wieman, 2011).

Keeping this in mind in the design of antihazing training, a single PowerPoint presentation with little or no discussion may have a limited influence on participants (Waldron, 2012). Instead, methods that promote active learning—such as instructor-directed or small-group discussions, class activities, and quizzes—should be strongly considered.

Frequency of Training

The association between training timing and frequency and the development of knowledge, attitudes and perceptions, and behaviors and skills remains unclear. Scholars recommend providing antihazing training early in a career, which can communicate the organization's lack of tolerance for hazing to new members (Allan and Madden, 2008; Hoover, 1999; Langford, 2008). However, as noted in interviews with subject-matter experts, just one training session at a point early in a career will likely have a limited effect on thoughts and behaviors after a certain time.[10] Thus, antihazing training should occur at multiple points in a career; some suggest annually.[11]

Alternatively, others suggest providing antihazing training at distinct developmental career levels to address new responsibilities and experiences arising as career responsibilities change.[12] As discussed previously, this should include leader training for identifying, preventing, and intervening in hazing. Overall, leaders must demonstrate commitment and support for antihazing initiatives, and this commitment may be fostered during well-designed training sessions.

Current Hazing Training in the Armed Forces

To help us better understand current antihazing training in the armed forces, representatives of each of the military services and the military service academies provided materials that described and/or contained

---

10 Interview with Susan Lipkins, March 5, 2014, and Norm Pollard, March 11, 2014.

11 Interview with Charles Hall, March 6, 2014.

12 Interview with Judy Van Raalte, March 5, 2014.

the content they provided their members about hazing at the time of our research in 2014.

For two reasons, this section focuses on the material that representatives of the active components provided us. First, representatives from the reserves and U.S. National Guard indicated that their antihazing training would follow that of the active components, so we considered the training materials the active components provided to be representative. Second, although we interviewed academy representatives to determine whether they had innovative training on hazing that could be adapted for use across the armed forces, the materials and information obtained did not suggest that the service academies are providing information that differs significantly from what the rest of the armed forces are providing. Therefore, this section focuses on the materials provided to active service members who are not attending the academies.

These materials included PowerPoint files, instructor manuals, course descriptions, videos, and pamphlets.[13] We developed a list of key factors on which to evaluate the provided training materials. These factors were based on the previously described individual-level antihazing efforts. Categories considered included the targeted audience, the frequency of training, the content of the training, and the mode of training (e.g., active and passive techniques). We drew on previous research and theory to define the factors that were to be rated within the provided materials. Two researchers then developed a coding scheme to assist with rating the extent to which the training materials provided evidence of each of the factors, or categories, of interest (see Appendix C for more details on the coding methodology).

Training Standardization and Frequency

The provided training materials showed variation among the military services in standardization and frequency of hazing training. The Coast Guard, Navy, and USMC provide training sessions that focus

[13] Standardized antihazing training was not available for the USMC. Instead, representatives provided a PowerPoint presentation deemed to be representative of the training that marines receive and responded to questions regarding antihazing training in the USMC.

exclusively on hazing. However, the Air Force and Army consider the topic of hazing within training efforts that are designed to address general negative behaviors, including equal opportunity–focused training. Thus, for example, several slides within a larger PowerPoint presentation addressed the topic of hazing. Further, the Air Force, Army, and Coast Guard provide different antihazing training materials to officers and enlisted personnel, such that the training provided these two groups is tailored to each group. The Army and Coast Guard also provide different training for leaders than to those who are not in leadership positions. In contrast, the Navy provides standardized training for all personnel, and USMC training varies greatly, depending on unit or instructor discretion.

In terms of when information regarding hazing is provided, all the services provide antihazing information early in a service member's career (i.e., at entry). In addition, all the services provide training at regular career intervals. However, only the Coast Guard, Navy, and USMC provide annual antihazing training (see Table 4.1).

Table 4.1
Antihazing Training Structure in the Armed Forces

Training Structure	Air Force	Army	Coast Guard	Navy	Marine Corps
Hazing-specific training	Not present	Not present	Present	Present	Present
Separate officer and enlisted training	Present	Present	Present	Not present	Varies
Leader training	Not present	Present	Present	Not present	Varies
Provision: at entry	Present	Present	Present	Present	Present
Provision: at career intervals	Present	Present	Present	Present	Present
Provision: annually	Not present	Varies	Present	Present	Present

NOTE: "Varies" indicates that unit or instructor discretion determines training characteristic. The Reserves and U.S. National Guard are not included in this assessment since they indicated their training would be consistent with the active component.

Training Characteristics

In evaluating the characteristics of antihazing training, we considered several topics that address the objective of increasing knowledge. These include providing a thorough description of the antihazing policy, details on the characteristics of hazing, examples of acts of hazing, the full DoD definition of hazing, information on how hazing is disciplined, materials on how to report hazing (e.g., who to report to), and information on one's duty to report or address incidents of hazing (see Table 4.2). Generally, training materials from each service show moderate evidence that these topics are addressed. However, none of the services provides the full DoD definition of hazing, which includes the DoD examples of hazing, to training participants. In terms of presenting information that targets participants' attitudes toward and behav-

Table 4.2
Antihazing Training Characteristics in the Armed Forces

Training Characteristics	Air Force	Army	Coast Guard	Navy	Marine Corps
Policy description	2	2	2	3	2
Characteristics of hazing	1	2	1	3	1
Example hazing acts	2	2	2	1	3
Full DoD definition	1	1	1	1	1
How hazing disciplined	1	2	2	2	0
How to report	1	0	2	2	3
Duty to report/address	0	1	1	3	0
Attitudes: negative effects	0	1	1	2	0
Attitudes: misperceptions	0	0	1	2	0
Skills (e.g., critical thinking)	2	1	0	1	0

NOTES: 0 = No evidence, 1 = Limited evidence, 2 = Moderate evidence, 3 = A great deal of evidence. The Reserves and U.S. National Guard are not included in this assessment since they indicated their training would be consistent with the active component.

iors for addressing hazing, the provided training materials tended to show little to no evidence that these elements are considered. This suggests that the services focus on providing facts and information that may increase knowledge about hazing but do not present material to address attitudes, perceptions, skills, or behaviors. Thus, the training tends not to include the materials that are more likely to address the culture and promote behavioral inclinations to eliminate hazing.

Training Techniques

Lectures appear to be the preferred training technique across the armed forces for presenting information on hazing (see Table 4.3). Specifically, PowerPoint presentations on hazing topics are common. The armed forces thus appear to encourage passive learning during this training, which can be helpful for rapid communication of a large amount of information. However, use of instructor-led discussions, which may encourage greater active learning, varies across the services, with the Army and Navy training materials showing the strongest evidence of use of this technique. For example, instructor-led discussions within Army antihazing training include the following questions:

- What is hazing?
- How can you as unit leaders support traditions?
- What are some examples of hazing that you are aware of?

Table 4.3
Antihazing Training Techniques in the Armed Forces

Training Techniques	Air Force	Army	Coast Guard	Navy	Marine Corps
Lecture	3	3	3	3	3
Instructor-led discussion	1	3	2	3	0
Structured assessment	1	0	2	0	0
In-class activities	0	0	2	0	0

NOTES: 0 = No evidence, 1 = Limited evidence, 2 = Moderate evidence, 3 = A great deal of evidence. The Reserves and U.S. National Guard are not included in this assessment since they indicated their training would be consistent with the active component.

In addition, the Coast Guard possesses a structured self-assessment on hazing that can be presented to participants during or following antihazing training to encourage recall and review of information, and the Air Force provides a limited written assessment addressing general negative workplace behaviors. Across the armed forces, in-class activities are rare. However, the Coast Guard training includes presenting the class with a hazing scenario and having the class discuss it.

Potential Areas for Improvement in Armed Forces Antihazing Training

Currently, the targeting of antihazing training to certain groups, including leaders, varies across the armed forces. To provide continuous and comprehensive antihazing training, all the armed forces should consider regularly providing information and instruction targeted to certain groups, such as training that focuses on the needs and experiences of officers and training that focuses on the needs and experiences of enlisted personnel. Further, providing appropriate information may help leaders identify and address hazing behaviors within their units and thus help reduce these acts across the armed forces. Including additional training elements may be difficult, however, because the armed forces must educate officers and enlisted personnel on multiple topics in a short period. Hazing prevention and antihazing training topics could also be included in relevant existing training sequences.

Across groups, the objectives of training should include increasing knowledge, influencing attitudes and perceptions, and changing or developing behaviors and skills. The armed forces currently focus on addressing knowledge about hazing and hazing policies. Training materials should also include information that addresses evaluations of and behavioral inclinations toward hazing.

Further, use of teaching or training techniques that encourage active consideration of and engagement with the material may facilitate greater retention for a longer time. The services use active learning on a limited basis in their current antihazing training. Additional provision of instructor-asked questions that encourage critical thinking may promote more active learning. In addition, enhancing the lecture-based format with small-group discussion, class activities, and ungraded quizzes may also encourage active learning among participants.

Recommendations

Overall, scholars addressing prevention and response in varied areas, including antihazing efforts, recommend systematic planning efforts that begin by assessing current needs and assets, then address short- and long-term goals, build from research and theory, and incorporate evaluation (Bond and Hauf, 2007; Dick and Carey, 1990; Hage et al., 2007; Langford, 2008; Wandersman, 2009). Implementing a systematic initiative that incorporates and builds from continuous monitoring and assessment may improve the efficacy of antihazing prevention and response efforts in the armed forces.

Therefore, as a first step in developing a more-systematic response to hazing prevention, the armed forces should conduct a needs assessment. As recommended by antihazing scholars, this would include a local analysis that reviews the scope of hazing and initiation activities, factors that contribute to or reduce the risk of hazing within the local context, and resources that are currently available and that may be needed to facilitate a more-effective approach to hazing elimination (Crow, Ammon, and Phillips, 2013; Langford, 2008).

To be able to determine the effectiveness of an antihazing initiative or component of an antihazing initiative, the desired end results must be specified. The objectives must be identified, then the extent to which the objectives were met must be determined. Langford (2008) notes that objectives within a hazing initiative should be SMART—an acronym for *specific*, *measurable*, *achievable*, *relevant*, and *time bound*. Thus, the *specific* end results of each effort, including training, within the hazing initiative should be identified, and *measures* that address the identified objectives should be collected. Further, given the time, resources, and level of support, the expected results should be *achievable*, or feasible, and the factors most *relevant* to hazing should be addressed. A time frame for implementation and assessment of effects should be established. Finally, although antihazing scholars recommend including well-designed evaluations in antihazing efforts, none currently exist within the armed forces or among civilian organizations.

As reviewed in the earlier sections of this chapter, our review of the literature and armed forces training materials and our interviews with both representatives of the armed forces and antihazing scholars suggest that the armed forces' antihazing prevention and response efforts should address the following:

- at the organization level, antihazing programs should
  - Communicate antihazing policies and consequences.
  - Hold leaders accountable for preventing hazing and swiftly punishing hazing.
  - Ensure that there are options for reporting anonymously and outside the chain of command.
  - Maintain accurate records of hazing allegations and incidents.
  - Assign an office to provide service-level oversight.
- at the individual level, antihazing programs should
  - Be comprehensive and continuous.
  - Include a training sequence that increases knowledge, influences attitudes and perceptions, and changes or develops behaviors and skills.
  - Teach leaders how to identify and address hazing.
  - Incorporate active learning techniques.

Conclusion

Although little systematic research is available on the efficacy of hazing prevention and response efforts in the armed forces, information on related topics (e.g., bullying prevention, violence prevention, and sexual assault prevention) and recommendations from scholars can inform the efforts of the armed forces. This information suggests that the armed forces should consider a coordinated hazing prevention effort that considers both organization-level and individual-level factors, with individual-level efforts that incorporate consideration of knowledge, attitudes and perceptions, and skills and behaviors. By developing a more-systematic approach to hazing prevention and response, the services should be in a better position to effectively address and eliminate incidents of hazing across the armed forces.

CHAPTER FIVE

Understanding the Prevalence and Characteristics of Hazing Incidents

Understanding the scope of hazing in the armed forces is critical to determining how to address the issue in the future. Comprehensively tracking incidents of military hazing is a key component of establishing the issue's scope. This chapter focuses on examining the feasibility of a comprehensive hazing incident database, including the key data elements that should be tracked.

To address this objective, we reviewed current hazing incident tracking methods across DoD, identified examples of best practices for a potential DoD-wide hazing database, identified key hazing incident data elements to track, and explored additional potential hazing measures that could be implemented across DoD. It is important to note that all recommendations we offer in response to this objective are predicated on the establishment of a standardized definition of hazing that can be clearly understood at all levels across the services, as discussed in Chapter Two.

The Importance of Tracking Hazing Incidents

Both our interviews with leading hazing experts and the literature on hazing prevention emphasize that, to fully understand the scope of a hazing problem, hazing incidents must be consistently tracked to replace anecdotal evidence with descriptive statistics (Fields, Collins, and Comstock, 2007; Johnson and Holman, 2004; Nuwer, 2001).

Knowing more about the scope and nature of hazing incidents can help identify trends and key factors associated with hazing incidents (e.g., types of individuals involved, locations, specific events or occasions where incidents are more likely to occur), which can, in turn, help inform prevention efforts and target appropriate resources to address the problem. To provide the most comprehensive picture of hazing within the military, tracking of reported hazing incidents should also be supplemented with anonymous surveys to capture unreported incidents of hazing. However, tracking reported hazing incidents may provide the greatest detail about the characteristics of hazing incidents, which can be used to identify trends and to inform prevention efforts.

We reviewed hazing prevention literature to assess the role of tracking hazing incidents in institutions outside DoD. While the literature in this area was limited and focused primarily on hazing at educational institutions, it did note that many organizations do not track hazing incidents (Nuwer, 2001). Often, no framework or structure is in place at an institution to do so. Additionally, there may be reluctance to report hazing incidents, on the part of both those involved in the incidents and the institutions' leaders, such as administrators at universities. Those involved in a hazing incident may not report it because they do not perceive hazing as a negative activity. Alternatively, they may fear retribution from the group initiating the hazing incident or may not be aware they were hazed because they did not understand what hazing is. In addition, leaders may be reluctant to report hazing incidents because of concerns about damaging the reputation of the organization or facing subsequent civil suits (Nuwer, 2001). Similar reporting and leadership concerns are likely to exist within the military. Therefore, these factors will be important to consider in establishing policy for comprehensive assessment of hazing incidents across DoD.

Tracking Hazing Incidents at the Service Level

Currently, hazing incidents are not tracked at the DoD level and are tracked at the individual service level only to a limited degree. In reports to Congress in July 2013, as required by Section 534 of the NDAA for FY 2013, the services were asked to provide estimates of the scope of the hazing problem:

- The Army reported that 130 incidents met the criteria for hazing between calendar year 2006 and March 2013.
- The Navy reported 111 total dispositions between the beginning of the second quarter of FY 2012 and the second quarter of FY 2013.
- USMC reported 98 total dispositions between May 2012 and May 2013.
- The Air Force reported 16 reports of hazing since 2000.
- The Coast Guard reported 14 cases of hazing investigated since 2007.

While these data provide some insight into the number of reported hazing incidents within DoD, the data's reliability and details on these incidents are limited. First, nonjudicial punishments are kept on file for only a limited time, so the numbers cannot be verified. Additionally, as this chapter will show, at the time of this study, many services did not track hazing incidents consistently, and prior to the congressional inquiry, most services did not track them as a distinct category in any database. Thus, while the data the services provided Congress offer something of a picture of the number of reported hazing incidents in the services, the data have limited reliability and comprehensiveness.

To begin examining the feasibility of and key data elements for a potential DoD-wide hazing incident database, we first reviewed and tried to understand the services' current hazing tracking methods. To do so, we interviewed service representatives who are members of the Hazing Review Team, aiming to understand the current methods the services are using to track hazing incidents, identify the data elements that are being tracked, and assess any potential challenges in developing a DoD-wide hazing database.

Current Service Tracking Methods

The services have varied methods of tracking hazing, with several of the services leveraging existing databases for tracking hazing incidents. As noted above, the services were required in 2013 to report to Congress on the status of hazing in their service, with one area specifically focusing on hazing incident tracking methods. In response to this request, most services have recently enhanced, or are working to enhance, their ability to comprehensively track hazing incidents. Most of the services with formal hazing tracking systems have recently established these systems or, as in the Army's case, are still in the process of developing these systems.

Below, we outline each service's methods for tracking, as described to us in the interviews we conducted in August 2013 and January 2014. The next section will provide a review of the capabilities of each service's tracking method using several key characteristics.

U.S. Army: Equal Opportunity Reporting System

At the time of our interviews, the Army was in the process of adding hazing incidents to its current equal opportunity reporting database. Prior to integrating hazing into the Equal Opportunity Reporting System (EORS), the Army did not formally track hazing incidents. The EORS will track hazing incidents using the same process currently used for discrimination complaints. Currently, the EORS contains a dropdown box from which the Equal Opportunity Advisor (EOA) can select the type of discrimination that has occurred, and the complaint will be classified accordingly. The Army intends for hazing to be an option in that dropdown box. The complainant will identify the incident as a hazing incident based on the Army's definition of hazing.

U.S. Navy: Military Equal Opportunity Network

In FY 2013, the Navy added hazing to its existing Military Equal Opportunity Network (MEONet) system.[1] The revised system, including hazing, launched in May 2013. In addition to hazing, MEONet

---

[1] The Navy is no longer using MEONet but is tracking hazing incidents and other complaints manually while working to identify a new system that will track incidents in a similar manner to MEONet.

tracks sexual harassment and equal opportunity complaints. The local command sends an official message when an incident occurs, and it is up to the discretion of the victim(s) and command whether or not an incident classifies as hazing. As with other types of complaints included in the system, EOAs are responsible for uploading hazing incidents into MEONet. The Navy is working to ensure that this system also includes incidents that are handled at the unit level.

U.S. Marine Corps: Discrimination and Sexual Harassment Database

The USMC added hazing to its Discrimination and Sexual Harassment (DASH) database in May 2013. DASH is a database owned by the equal opportunity community, which also tracks discrimination and sexual harassment complaints. In accordance with Marine Corps Order 1700.28B, two distinct mechanisms are used for the immediate and mandatory reporting of all hazing allegations. First, an Operations/Event Incident Report–3 Serious Incident Report must be submitted to the Marine Corps Operation Center within six hours of any alleged hazing incident or within six hours of receiving information about any alleged hazing incident. Commanding officers or officers in charge are then required to coordinate with the command EOA and ensure the associated DASH report is submitted to the Commandant of the Marine Corps Manpower Equal Opportunity Branch according to the established time lines for initial, continuation, and final reports. Initial DASH reports must be submitted within 72 hours of any alleged hazing incident or within 72 hours of becoming aware of any alleged hazing incident. Operations/Event Incident Report–3 Serious Incident Report is primarily a formal messaging system. To keep leadership informed about hazing incidents, the DASH system is the formal tracking system, which tracks incidents through final disposition. The USMC is currently modifying the DASH system to allow tracking unit and command information at the aggregate level.

U.S. Coast Guard: Coast Guard Investigative Service and Court-Martial Cases

The Coast Guard employs two systems that track hazing incidents in two separate phases, depending on the status of the incident. The Coast Guard Investigative Service (CGIS) tracks hazing incidents in the investigative phase. Once a CGIS case goes to court-martial, the incident enters the disciplinary phase and is tracked as a court-martial case. Incidents are tracked in CGIS once a complaint is elevated from the command level. If an incident is handled at the command level and is not investigated, it is currently not tracked. Starting a few years prior to this study, the Coast Guard has been flagging incidents that involve hazing and tracking them in these systems as such.

U.S. Air Force: Automated Military Justice Analysis and Management System

The Air Force does not formally track hazing incidents. Hazing incidents for which court-martial or nonjudicial punishment is being considered for potential UCMJ violations will appear in the Automated Military Justice Analysis and Management System. However, these incidents are not tracked specifically as hazing incidents. To attempt to identify incidents in the system that involve hazing behaviors, users can conduct a keyword search of the case narratives for *hazing* and related terms.

National Guard Bureau: Army and Air Force Inspector General Databases

The National Guard Bureau administers the U.S. National Guard, which consists of the Army National Guard and the Air National Guard. The National Guard Bureau does not formally track hazing incidents. Hazing incidents that are reported through the Army or Air Force Inspector General (IG) are tracked in either the Army or Air Force IG database under the "harassment and maltreatment" category. Harassment and maltreatment cases can be identified as having involved hazing by reading incident report text for references to hazing behavior. However, if a hazing incident is reported through another channel, it is not captured in the IG database.

Review of Service Tracking Systems

For the services that do have formal hazing incident tracking systems in place, or are in the process of establishing a formal system, we reviewed the tracking systems along six key characteristics:

- *The system is a standalone system for hazing.* The system is exclusively for tracking hazing incidents rather than being an existing database to which hazing was added. A standalone service-level database could be considered for potential adoption for DoD-wide use, if DoD opts to leverage an existing database. Additionally, Section 534 of the NDAA for FY 2013 asked the services to comment on the feasibility of establishing a new database to track incidents of hazing. While the services did not uniformly support such a database, we aimed to confirm whether any service had established a standalone database in response to this congressional interest.
- *Hazing is a standalone category in the database.* The database clearly flags hazing incidents and/or tracks them in a separate section. This does not include incidents retrievable only through word searches of incident reports. Difficulty in identifying hazing incidents when not specifically flagged may lead to incorrect estimates of the prevalence of reported hazing incidents.
- *The system tracks bullying separately.* The database identifies and tracks bullying incidents separately from hazing incidents. Research shows a distinction between hazing and bullying (Ostvik and Rudmin, 2001). Further, this distinction was raised several times during our study interviews and in discussion with the DoD Hazing Review Team. Given these discussions, military policy also seems to be trending toward a separate definition of bullying, leading to potential separate future reporting requirements for hazing and bullying. Therefore, we included this as a characteristic to examine based on potential future reporting requirements.
- *The system tracks anonymous reports.* The system can track anonymous reports of hazing incidents. As required by Section 534 of the NDAA for FY 2013, the services were asked to provide information about methods to track and report hazing incidents, including anonymous reports. Furthermore, the ability to make anonymous reports is recommended as a component of hazing prevention efforts.

- *The system tracks the incident from initial report to final disposition.* Incidents are tracked from the time of report, through the investigation process, and any disciplinary proceedings. This allows trend analysis at each stage of the hazing incident case.
- *The system tracks all allegations of hazing.* All allegations of hazing are tracked, not just substantiated incidents. Tracking all allegations of hazing provides a more comprehensive assessment of potential hazing incidents and promotes tracking consistency across the services.

Table 5.1 outlines where the six characteristics are present in the service tracking methods.

As Table 5.1 illustrates, no service has a standalone database to track hazing. All current and pending tracking methods in the armed forces have involved adding hazing to an existing database originally

Table 5.1
Characteristics of Current Service Tracking Methods

Characteristic	Army[a]	Navy	Marine Corps	Coast Guard
The system is exclusively for hazing				
Hazing is a standalone category in the database	✓	✓	✓	✓
The system tracks bullying separately	✓			
The system tracks anonymous reports	✓	✓		
The system tracks the incident from initial report to final disposition	✓	✓	✓	
The system tracks all allegations of hazing	✓	✓	✓	

NOTE: The Air Force and U.S. National Guard were not included in this assessment because they do not formally track hazing incidents.

[a] Our assessment of the Army hazing incident tracking methods was based on the planned tracking system that is currently under development.

developed for a different purpose. In such databases, hazing incidents are tagged or tracked in a separate section of the database for all services assessed. At the time of this study, in 2014, only the Army intended to track bullying incidents separately in its EORS database. Other services currently either do not track bullying incidents or do not differentiate between hazing and bullying incidents. The Navy's MEONet and Army's EORS will allow the tracking of anonymous reports, while the Coast Guard and USMC systems do not. USMC representatives noted in interviews that the assistance, protections, and support services designated for victims and witnesses of hazing have so far precluded the development and implementation of anonymous reporting procedures. The Army, Navy, and USMC systems track the full life cycle of hazing incidents, from initial report to final disposition. Additionally, these three services' systems track all allegations of hazing, rather than just those that have been substantiated. The nature of the Coast Guard's two tracking systems, through CGIS and court-martial cases, means that they track only the incidents that reach the levels of formal investigation and the disciplinary process. Thus, although the services have started to implement tracking systems, there is inconsistency across the service-specific systems, and several areas could be improved.

Key Data Elements

Currently, the services are not tracking hazing incidents in similar ways. Interviews with service representatives revealed examples of hazing incident elements tracked:

- name, unit, date of incident, description of incident, and status of the case
- gender, rank, race, and brief summary of the incident; whether incident was verbal, physical, or psychological; and outcome in terms of any punishment
- information on the victim or complaintants and offenders, time of incident, location of incident, name of investigating officer, results of the investigation, and how incident was adjudicated.

While the services should continue to improve their ability to track hazing incidents within their own ranks, it is also important to establish a tracking method that permits comparisons across services. This will allow a DoD-wide assessment of the issue. To improve its understanding of the scope of hazing across the armed forces and ensure data and reporting consistency across the different services, DoD must also establish standardized data elements for tracking. Standardized tracking of certain elements will allow trends or characteristics of hazing incidents to emerge and can help inform prevention and training efforts.

We interviewed hazing experts in academia in addition to service representatives from the Hazing Review Team to identify potential key elements for tracking that DoD should consider. These elements can help to identify trends in hazing incidents that could aid in prevention and provide DoD with a more-comprehensive picture of the scope of hazing taking place across the services. These interviews led to a list of proposed key data elements for DoD consideration:

- demographics of victim(s) and alleged perpetrator(s)
- location type (e.g., whether ship or shore)
- characteristics of hazing incident circumstances (e.g., whether the incident stemmed from a ceremony, whether alcohol was involved)
- types of behaviors involved to use as examples for training (e.g., physical, verbal, or psychological)
- severity of hazing incident (e.g., subtle versus violent; mild, moderate, or severe).

Interviewees also suggested that DoD consider including process elements for each reported hazing incident. These could include time lapse between incident occurrence and reporting; investigation information, such as when the alleged perpetrator(s) and witnesses were questioned; and outcomes, such as whether or not the allegation of hazing was substantiated and any subsequent relevant actions including punishment.

Tracking these types of elements may help prevent hazing by, for example, identifying trends in terms of demographics and location that could help the services target hazing prevention efforts. Additionally, characteristics of the hazing incident's circumstances and the types of behaviors involved could provide relevant example hazing behaviors to include in hazing training prevention materials. If DoD opts to include an element related to the severity of the hazing incident, it must work with the services to define the levels of severity. This will ensure uniform understanding and tracking. There should be clear definitions for each "level" of hazing, so that the individual receiving the report is clear about how it should be categorized. DoD may also decide to define severity of the hazing incidents according to its consequences or outcomes.

Potential DoD-Wide Hazing Database

Given the current lack of uniformity in tracking hazing incidents at the service level at the time of this study, we explored the feasibility of creating a comprehensive hazing database at the DoD level that would incorporate hazing incident data from each of the services. A DoD-wide hazing database would define elements for tracking, remedying standardization issues at the service level, and would promote accurate and consistent reporting. We interviewed service representatives to gain insights into the issues related to the establishment of a DoD-wide hazing database. Additionally, we identified existing relevant DoD-wide databases that may serve as examples of best practices, should DoD opt to establish a hazing incident database at the DoD level.

In interviews, service representatives outlined benefits of and challenges to establishing a DoD-wide hazing database. Representatives from all the services agreed that a DoD-wide system would streamline efforts, eliminating the need for service-specific tracking of hazing. Additionally, interviewees stated that a DoD system would standardize tracking elements and become the department's system of record. However, they also identified challenges, which mainly related to the resources required to establish the database and to ensuring the protection of personally identifiable information.

Best Practice Examples

To identify options for a comprehensive database, we first explored methods of tracking discipline and/or punishment to leverage for tracking hazing incidents. Our review included IG websites, the Defense Case Activity Tracking System, and court-martial databases. However, we found that none of these tracking methods provides a model for a DoD-wide hazing incident database. Some of these systems, such as court-martial databases, are tracked at the service level, and systems at the DoD level did not appear to aggregate service-level data in a manner that would be relevant to comprehensively tracking hazing incidents.

We then reviewed databases beyond those focused on discipline and punishment to identify databases that could exemplify best practices for a potential DoD-wide hazing incident database. Many of the databases identified for review were suggested by service representatives from the Hazing Review Team. The systems we reviewed and considered for more in-depth examination included the following:

- *Defense Sexual Assault Incident Database (DSAID).* DSAID is the department's system of record for reporting sexual assaults, tracking incidents at the DoD level.
- *Recovery Coordination Program Support Solution (RCP-SS).* RCP-SS is a tool for recovery care coordinators providing support to wounded, ill, and injured service members. The tool coordinates care management, comprehensive needs assessment, and comprehensive recovery plans and operates at the DoD level.
- *Marine Corps Recruiting Information Support System.* This USMC-only enterprise-level system automates administrative procedures for USMC recruiting station operations.
- *Alcohol and Drug Management Information Tracking System.* This Navy-only database management system tracks information about personnel treated at Navy nonmedical facilities for abuse of drugs or alcohol.
- *Armed Forces Medical Examiner System.* This system primarily tracks medical-legal examinations on military and civilian per-

sonnel who are killed or die in a combat zone. This system operates at the DoD level.

From this review, we identified DSAID and RCP-SS as the databases most appropriate for more in-depth examination and as possible examples of best practices for a DoD-wide hazing incident database. We chose them because they both track data at the DoD level and have relevant content of limited scope. We interviewed representatives from the Sexual Assault and Prevention Office (SAPRO) and Office of Warrior Care Policy to discuss their process for standing up and maintaining DSAID and RCP-SS, respectively, and to learn more in-depth information about the databases and their potential applicability for a DoD-wide hazing database. Specific discussion questions covered the following:

- the process for standing up the database and overall costs associated
- data elements currently tracked in the database
- the process for establishing common data elements across the services
- the potential benefits of a DoD-wide tracking database versus service-specific tracking systems
- lessons learned from standing up a DoD-wide database that DoD should be aware of if moving forward with a DoD-wide hazing database.

We next provide more details about each of these systems.

The Defense Sexual Assault Incident Database

DSAID supports service Sexual Assault Prevention and Response (SAPR) program management and SAPRO. DSAID was established in FY 2012 to meet congressional requirements outlined in the FY 2009 NDAA. Specifically, Section 563 of the FY 2009 NDAA mandates the implementation of a centralized, case-level database for collection and maintenance of information about sexual assaults involving members of the armed forces. Following this legislation, the SAPR Data Collection and Reporting Working Group, with membership across the services, was stood up to work toward meeting this requirement. The working group submitted a DoD SAPR data collection and reporting system concept design report in January 2009 that outlined the current environment for sexual assault reporting at the service level, as well as recommended the concept and requirements for a DoD SAPR data collection and reporting system (DoD, 2009). This report represented a collaborative effort from the services to establish this new reporting system.

DSAID cost $11 million to develop and implement and costs approximately $1 million annually for operation and maintenance. DSAID's capabilities include

- case management: inputting and maintaining data pertaining to sexual assault cases and tracking support to sexual assault victims throughout the life cycle of a case
- business management: documenting case management reviews to facilitate Sexual Assault Response Coordinator and service SAPR program manager administration and management
- ad hoc queries and reporting: producing automated, congressionally mandated reports and ad hoc queries to allow data analysis and trend identification and support program planning analysis and management.

The data elements DSAID tracks include victim, incident, subject demographic, subject disposition, and SAPR program administration. SAPRO also established the Change Control Board, a working group with representation across the services, to serve as a communication and oversight tool once DSAID was established. Any potential changes to DSAID must be communicated to this board such that its members understand the effects on the system, the level of effort involved, and the cost associated and can provide feedback.

According to SAPRO representatives, the implementation of DSAID benefited DoD in several ways. The database provides accurate, standardized reporting on sexual assault incidents, encouraging transparency of data while ensuring privacy. This standardization and common tracking system has also increased communication across the services regarding sexual assault. Establishment of DSAID has decreased the services' operations and maintenance costs: No longer needing their legacy systems, the services voluntarily shut them down. Training efforts were also consolidated at the DoD level.

Recovery Coordination Program Support Solution

RCP-SS is an automated tool that supports the processes of enrolling, identifying, and managing the nonclinical needs of recovering service members and their families. It is overseen by the Office of Warrior Care Policy and provides an automated case management tracking system. RCP-SS was established in FY 2010 to meet requirements outlined in Section 1611 of the FY 2008 NDAA and Directive-Type Memorandum 08-049, which included policy mandates on improvements to the care, management, and transition of recovering service members and on the creation of an automated tool for the Comprehensive Recovery Plan, which outlines service members' recovery goals and the resources needed to achieve them. RCP-SS automates the case management process, replacing the paper-based files used prior to the system's development, promoting a smooth transition for service members from locations among services and exit from a service, as well as ensuring accurate and standardized data for reporting. The system cost less than $1.5 million to build and develop and costs approximately $500,000 annually for operation and maintenance.

RCP-SS streamlines recovering service member support processes, reducing redundant data and processing time for care coordination activities. The system also facilitates collaboration across the services, OSD, and the Department of Veterans Affairs for integrated case management by providing the ability to share case information across programs while ensuring privacy. RCP-SS promotes uniformity across programs as a single-source application for case management users, facilitating accurate data reporting and access. RCP-SS developers identified data elements for inclusion in the system based on existing paper forms used by the services, designed to meet NDAA requirements. The Office of Warrior Care Policy worked closely with the case managers from each service to develop RCP-SS, engaging with the system users and building the system with their input. This "technical working group" has been maintained to connect with system users and engage them in system development and any future modifications.

The system tracks elements related to enrollment and identifying and managing service member and family needs. Within each case, the following elements are included: service member information, category assignment, acuity assessment, enrollment (includes spouse and dependent demographics, power of attorney, command, service information, awards, education and training, DoD and Department of Veterans Affairs recovery team members, incident or injury information, and medical administration information), needs assessment, recovery plan with goals, needs and actions, case attachments (document management specific to the case), and contract details (case notes).

Lessons Learned

Representatives from DSAID and RCP-SS offered the lessons they learned in standing up a DoD-wide database that DoD should consider for a potential hazing incident database. These lessons emphasized communication as critical to any DoD-wide tracking effort. Both DSAID and RCP-SS representatives stressed the need to establish and maintain a working group with representation across the services. This working group should be used to ensure frequent and sustained communication throughout the database development process, as well as for potential system modifications over time. Additionally, DSAID and RCP-SS representatives strongly suggested that system end users be engaged early in the development process and continue to be engaged for continued system modifications. While the DoD or federal perspective is important, it should also be augmented with the perspective of the system end user, which will provide a more comprehensive assessment of system requirements.

On the technical side, DSAID and RCP-SS representatives reported that identifying the appropriate hosting environment for the database system early in the process was key. Considerations for the hosting environment include its cost and whether it is government certified. For example, RCP-SS was currently in the process of moving its hosting environment to the Defense Information Systems Agency, where the system would have its own servers and could be expanded as needed, which the system did not have previously. While this will improve the system's capabilities, migrating a system from one hosting facility to another has significant costs and is something to consider early in the development process for a database. DSAID and RCP-SS representatives also emphasized the importance of choosing a flexible platform to support development and system modifications. This is particularly important because congressional requirements may change, and the system must be modified accordingly. DSAID representatives elected to use a commercial-off-the-shelf product for their system. The risk of this option is that the code is proprietary to the contractor rather than DoD. If DoD instead develops its own platform for the database, DoD would own the code. However, commercial-off-the-shelf products are built on a proven structure and allow rapid deployment. It is also important to consider the time and cost associated with each option.

Finally, both DSAID and RCP-SS representatives recommended analyzing the historical and current environment before embarking on developing a new system, to ensure that no existing system has the same capabilities or can be leveraged to meet the desired system's needs. Representatives also pointed out that, if an existing system has the same capabilities, the new system will not be able to receive a System of Record Notice. This notice, published in the *Federal Register*, is required for all systems tracking or maintaining personal information about individuals.

Recommendations for a DoD-Wide Hazing Database

If DoD chooses to spend the required time and resources on developing a DoD-wide hazing database, examples exist to guide that process. DSAID, in particular, offers a clear roadmap for development because of the similar nature of its content (i.e., incidents of negative behavior) and its usage goals (e.g., standardization in tracking, reporting to Congress). However, some services have recently established comprehensive tracking systems to answer congressional inquiries, which required time and resources to develop. At this time, it may be more feasible to leverage these investments at the service level and modify existing systems to ensure that uniform data elements are tracked across the services. This would avoid duplication of effort at the DoD level and save on additional time and resource requirements. Additionally, DoD does not currently have a clear understanding of the scope of the hazing problem or a well-defined definition, which is needed for accurate tracking. Once the DoD has a clear definition for hazing and is able to uniformly track hazing incidents and better assess the scope of hazing across the services, it can then better determine whether to invest in a DoD-wide database system or whether service-level tracking remains sufficient.

Measuring Hazing Through Surveys

In evaluating methods for tracking hazing, we explored alternative measures to assess the hazing problem beyond those that track reported incidents. An assessment of hazing through anonymous surveys offers an assessment that is distinct from that provided by incident tracking and can produce a more-comprehensive picture of the scope of the hazing problem. For example, a survey can assess knowledge about the definition and characteristics of hazing and about attitudes toward hazing. Anonymous surveys can also more accurately identify the occurrence of hazing behaviors without necessarily relying on service members to identify the behaviors as "hazing." As discussed earlier, service members do not always view hazing behaviors as "negative" because they are often associated with rites of passage and because individuals sometimes do not understand the definition of hazing. Surveys can focus on specific examples of behaviors and limit bias regarding attitudes toward hazing more generally. Finally, given that individuals may be apprehensive of coming forward and reporting incidents, the use of a confidential or anonymous survey may help provide a more-accurate estimate of the prevalence of hazing than could be found only through tracking of formally reported incidents.

Current DoD Hazing Survey Efforts

Currently, hazing is not a standard topic area assessed on DoD-wide surveys. However, DoD survey organizations have done preliminary work to measure hazing. For example, the Defense Equal Opportunity Management Institute (DEOMI) has developed the following survey items as part of the revised 2014 DEOMI Organizational Climate Survey (DEOCS):

- Newcomers are harassed or humiliated prior to being accepted into the organization.
- To be accepted in this organization, members must participate in potentially dangerous activities not related to mission.
- Newcomers in this organization are dared to engage in potentially harmful activities not related to mission.[2]

While these survey items provide an initial step into assessing hazing, these items are fairly broad and do not provide specific example behaviors. Additionally, the DEOCS does not sample the force in a manner that permits drawing conclusions about the entire force. However, the DEOCS could be used to assess the presence of hazing at the unit level.

Defense Manpower Data Center (DMDC) surveys may also include hazing-related questions in the near future. DMDC's survey sampling methods are designed to be representative of the entire force and provide one kind of DoD-wide hazing assessment. However, the DMDC hazing survey measures that are currently in development focus on experiences with hazing due to association with a particular demographic group. Because of this focus on hazing experiences driven by demographic group identity, these measures will not provide an entire-force picture of hazing.

Thus, although DEOMI and DMDC have made initial efforts to assess hazing through survey measures, these items will likely not accurately assess the prevalence of hazing across the DoD.

Recommendations for DoD Hazing Survey Efforts

As a complement to tracking of hazing incidents, we recommend that DoD also survey service members in a manner that provides a compre-

2 For more information on the DEOCS, see the DEOMI website.

hensive assessment of hazing and is representative of the entire force. A review of the literature on hazing and hazing surveys used at colleges and high schools revealed that no standard survey hazing measure has been established. Instead, surveys that assess hazing are tailored to the specific context of the population being sampled. In most cases, this has been the high school or college context. Examples include

- National Survey of Sports Teams: In 1999, Alfred University conducted a national survey of college athletes, coaches, and staff at NCAA institutions that examined initiation rites for athletics (Hoover, 1999).
- National Study of Student Hazing: In 2005–2007, researchers from Maine University conducted a survey of 11,482 students from more than 50 colleges and universities (Allan and Madden, 2008).

Additionally, Pershing (2006) examined data from a GAO survey given to U.S. Naval Academy midshipmen in 1990 that included questions pertaining to experiences with and perceptions of hazing at the academy.

Given the need to tailor survey items to the specific context, hazing literature and literature regarding survey measures of other negative behaviors, such as sexual assault, can provide principles that DoD can use to develop hazing survey items. For example, research on sexual assault finds that survey measures that use the word "rape" tend to produce much smaller, and presumably less accurate, prevalence estimates compared with surveys that use behaviorally specific questions to describe sexual assault (e.g., Fisher, 2009; Tjaden and Thoennes, 1998). Surveys developed to assess hazing have followed a similar pattern, providing behavior-specific examples for participants to rate instead of using the term *hazing* in the survey items, which may bias some individuals from responding. The inability to include an exhaustive list of hazing behaviors is a notable limitation of course. Therefore, the services should agree to some extent on the behavioral items included in the survey so that survey results are relevant across the armed forces.

Thus, in developing a survey tool to better assess the prevalence of hazing across the services, we offer the following recommendations:

- Survey participation should be confidential or anonymous to ensure respondents feel they can be open and honest when answering the survey questions.
- Survey items should not ask specifically about experiences using the term *hazing*. There is no clear understanding of what hazing includes, and there is also the potential for bias—for instance, some may view hazing as a positive "rite of passage" activity.
- Rather than referring specifically to hazing, survey items should elicit more-reliable responses by using example behaviors. The example behaviors for the survey should be based on behaviors that have been identified as the most prevalent types of hazing in the services. Data on these behaviors can be collected through several different sources, including interviews, focus groups, and analysis of reported incidents.
- DoD should also consider including survey items related to attitudes toward hazing, which can then help inform prevention efforts.

Conclusion

A comprehensive assessment of hazing must include a database that tracks reported hazing incidents across the DoD. Understanding that not all incidents of hazing will be reported, confidential or anonymous surveys should also be used to supplement reported incident databases to give a more-comprehensive assessment of hazing across the services. These methods of data collection will provide two distinct types of data related to hazing.

If DoD chooses to move forward with the development of a DoD-level hazing database, best practice examples exist to provide a roadmap for development. However, at this time, it may be more practical to track at the service level because of cost and resource restrictions and lack of clarity regarding the extent of the hazing problem across the armed forces. Many services have also already invested in establishing methods for tracking hazing incidents, while similar efforts have not been made at the OSD level. DoD should work with the services to establish uniform tracking elements and leverage existing databases at the service level to track hazing incidents along these standardized elements. Once DoD has a better understanding of the scope of the hazing problem, it may choose to reassess the need for a DoD-wide tracking system and whether the associated investment is worthwhile. Once hazing incidents are more consistently tracked at the service level, the magnitude of reported hazing incidents will become apparent and can help inform the decision about whether or not a DoD-level database is warranted to further assess and track these incidents.

Current DoD survey measures of hazing may not adequately assess the full range of hazing activities or reach a DoD-wide audience. Refinement of these survey measures to assess hazing more accurately and including them in DoD-wide surveys that are representative of the entire force can help provide a broader and more-accurate assessment of hazing across the armed forces.

CHAPTER SIX

Conclusions and Recommendations

In an effort to help the DoD build a more-systematic approach to hazing prevention and response across the armed forces, this report has included an assessment of the current DoD hazing definition, a review of theory and research on why hazing occurs, a review of recommended practices for preventing and responding to hazing, and an examination of the feasibility of and key data elements for a comprehensive hazing incident database. In this chapter, we build from this information and present our overall conclusions and recommendations.

Defining Hazing

Given that confusion often exists about which actions constitute hazing and which do not, a well-understood and well-publicized definition of hazing in the military is critical. This definition may help the military address hazing, for example, by encouraging reviews of currently sanctioned or allowed activities in light of the definition. Our review of the scholarly literature and critiques of other hazing laws and definitions indicated that DoD's current definition of hazing includes two key components that should continue to be part of any revised hazing definition: (1) that hazing can be psychological and not just involve physical contact and (2) that the consent of the victim does not eliminate the culpability of hazers.

We recommend the following improvements to DoD's definition of hazing:

- Include qualities that are distinctive to hazing, to distinguish it from other types of abuse and mistreatment. For example, it should be noted that hazing activities are often part of initiations, intended to maintain group membership, or part of a change in status or position within a group.
- Clarify the role of authority figures and the individual's responsibility to address authority-approved hazing. This will help eliminate ambiguity about the culpability of those who engage in authority-sanctioned hazing.
- Consider the use of more-objective terms in describing harm, such as "psychological injury" or "extreme mental stress." These may be used in addition to, or as alternatives to, "humiliating" or "demeaning." The terms used should be clear and specific about the psychological consequences of interest.
- Ensure that the list of examples is based on hazing acts considered to be prevalent within the military today. These could be drawn from recently prosecuted or reported hazing acts or could be based on perceptions of prevalence from service members. These examples can also be used to differentiate hazing from sanctioned rituals and training exercises. As part any service-specific policies or training, each service may also want to tailor the examples to the acts most common in the particular service.[1]

These revisions are intended to help address possible uncertainty about hazing among military personnel. Additionally, a clearer, more-objective definition of hazing should help improve reporting and tracking of hazing incidents.

Why Hazing Occurs

Hazing is often described as involving abuse of potential and new members of a group (it may also include some maltreatment of cur-

[1] Since completion of this study, the DoD Hazing Review Team has drafted a revised definition for hazing that incorporates many of these recommendations. The revised definition will be included in new DoD hazing policy.

rent members) by a more-senior cohort with the goal of bringing the new members into the group. It is a common practice across different countries, cultures, and societies, and hazing or similar ritualistic behaviors have been practiced for centuries (Cimino, 2011; Sosis, 2004). Proponents of hazing argue that acts of hazing or harsh initiation rituals contribute to increased liking of, commitment to, and cohesion with the group. However, evidence for these different effects is mixed, and research and reports demonstrate that hazing can lead to physical and psychological injuries among hazees (Finkel, 2002). Theory and research suggest that individuals endure hazing to signal their commitment to group members and, thus, to receive the benefits of group membership. In addition, hazers may use hazing to eliminate free riders and maintain power differentials within the group.

Because the military is a very hierarchical organization in which individuals operate as highly cooperative teams, often in high-risk environments, hazing incidents may be more likely. Further, in a context with various sanctioned initiations and rituals, it may be particularly difficult to understand when an activity constitutes hazing. The recommendations we describe in this chapter are designed to help DoD begin to build a foundation for a more-systematic approach to hazing prevention and response that may be better able to address some of the uncertainty, confusion, and attitudes toward hazing that make it difficult to eliminate.

Preventing and Responding to Hazing in the Armed Forces

As a first step in developing a more-systematic response to hazing prevention, the armed forces may wish to conduct a needs assessment, including a review of the scope of hazing and initiation activities, the factors that contribute to or reduce the risk of hazing in the local context, and the resources that are currently available and that may be needed to facilitate a more-effective approach to hazing elimination. This may also include a review of currently sanctioned, or allowed, activities to ensure they do not constitute hazing. In addition, the desired end results of an antihazing program must be specified, and a time frame for implementation and assessment of effects should be established.

We identified several broad areas that should be addressed within the armed forces' antihazing prevention and response efforts:

- at the organization level, antihazing programs should
  - Communicate antihazing policies and consequences.
  - Hold leaders accountable for preventing hazing and swiftly punishing hazing.
  - Ensure that there are options for reporting anonymously and outside the chain of command.
  - Maintain accurate records of hazing allegations and incidents.
  - Assign an office to provide service-level oversight.
- at the individual level, antihazing programs should
  - Be comprehensive and continuous.
  - Include a training sequence that increases knowledge, influences attitudes and perceptions, and changes or develops behaviors and skills.
  - Teach leaders how to identify and address hazing.
  - Incorporate active learning techniques.

Understanding the Prevalence and Characteristics of Hazing Incidents

One key limitation of DoD's efforts to combat hazing is that we do not have a good sense of the scope of the hazing problem across DoD. To effectively address hazing in the military, DoD and the services need to understand the scope of hazing within their ranks. We reviewed current hazing-incident tracking methods across DoD, assessed the feasibility of a potential DoD-wide hazing database to track hazing incidents, and identified ways that the armed forces can improve the tracking of hazing incidents, albeit with some limitations remaining.

In examining the services' current systems for tracking hazing incidents, we found that, although many of the services have started to implement methods to track reported incidents of hazing, there is inconsistency across the service-specific systems and several areas that could be improved. Furthermore, the Air Force and U.S. National Guard do not formally track hazing incidents.

Feasibility of a DoD-Wide Hazing Database

Given the current lack of uniformity in tracking hazing incidents at the service level and the lack of comprehensive tracking systems in some of the services, we explored the feasibility of creating a comprehensive hazing database at the DoD level that would standardize and incorporate hazing incident data from each of the services. We identified the DSAID and RCP-SS database, two databases that track data at the DoD level and have relevant content of limited scope, as offering some best practices for a possible DoD-wide hazing database.

Ultimately, however, we recommend leveraging the investments already made in the existing service-level databases and continuing to improve these systems, rather than developing a new, DoD-level database at this time. Existing service systems could be modified to ensure that uniform data elements are tracked across the services. This would avoid duplication of effort at the DoD level and save on additional time and resource requirements. Additionally, DoD does not currently have a clear understanding of the scope of the hazing problem. Once DoD has a better understanding of the scope of the hazing problem, it can better determine whether it should invest in a DoD-wide database or whether service-level tracking remains sufficient.

From interviews with hazing experts in academia and service representatives from the Hazing Review Team, we also identified the following key elements for tracking that DoD should consider establishing:

- demographics of victim(s) and alleged perpetrator(s)
- location type (e.g., whether ship or shore)
- characteristics of hazing incident circumstances (e.g., whether the incident stemmed from a ceremony, whether alcohol was involved)
- types of behaviors involved to use as examples for training (e.g., physical, verbal, or psychological)

- severity of hazing incident (e.g., subtle versus violent; mild, moderate, or severe)
- investigative process elements (e.g., length of time for investigation; whether the allegation was substantiated; the outcome of the report, including punishment).

Measuring Hazing Through Surveys

To complement any formal tracking system, we also recommend that DoD survey the force in a manner that provides a more-comprehensive assessment of hazing and is representative of the entire force:

- Survey participation should be confidential or anonymous to ensure respondents feel they can be open and honest when answering the survey questions.
- Survey items should not ask specifically about experiences with the term *hazing*. There is no clear understanding of what hazing includes, and there is also potential for bias; for instance, some may view hazing as a positive "rite of passage" activity.
- Rather than referring specifically to hazing, survey items should elicit more-reliable responses by using example behaviors. These example behaviors should be based on the behaviors that have been identified as the most prevalent types of hazing in the services. Data on these behaviors can be collected from several different sources, including interviews, focus groups, and analysis of reported incidents.
- DoD should also consider including survey items related to attitudes toward hazing, which can then help inform prevention efforts.

Conclusion

Rites of passage and initiation rituals have long been part of U.S. military culture. However, along with these activities have often come acts of hazing in which individuals are subjected to abusive treatment that goes beyond sanctioned ceremonies in an effort to solidify commitment to the group and/or its structure. In recent years, more-extreme cases of alleged hazing have led to the high-profile deaths of several service members, renewing the interest of the public and Congress in eliminating these hazing rituals from military culture. The recommendations documented in this report provide an initial foundation for the DoD to begin to develop a more-systematic approach to preventing and responding to hazing across the armed forces.

APPENDIX A

Overview of Study Methodology

This appendix provides greater detail on our methodological approach for addressing each of the study objectives.

Review of DoD and Service-Level Policies and Practices

To better understand current hazing related policies and practices across the armed forces, we reviewed current DoD and service policy documents published online, as well as documents that service representatives on the Hazing Review Team and our sponsors at the Office of Diversity Management and Equal Opportunity shared with us. This review included examining the services' current methods for tracking hazing incidents, as well as their hazing prevention education and training materials.

We also conducted semistructured interviews with representatives of the military services, including the Guard and Reserves, who served on the Hazing Review Team, as well as representatives of each of the military service academies. Interviews lasted approximately 30 to 45 minutes. During these interviews, we asked representatives for information on relevant hazing policy and practices, including information on any antihazing training and education provided and on systems for tracking hazing incidents.

Review of the Scientific Literature

We used several strategies to locate research and literature relevant to addressing the study research tasks. First, we conducted electronic searches for articles and books from a variety of relevant databases, including PsycINFO, EBSCOhost's Military & Government Collection, Academic Search Complete, Education Resources Information Center, Google Scholar, and the databases of the Defense Technical Information Center and the GAO. We also conducted general Google searches using relevant keywords and phrases. These searches focused on finding literature on military hazing, sports hazing, hazing in fraternities and sororities, college hazing, hazing among paramilitary groups, the causes and consequences of hazing, and the relationship between bullying and hazing. For example, searches combined the keyword *hazing* with *military*, *soldiers*, *Army*, *war*, *combat*, *training*, *academy*, or *unit*. In reviewing the literature on practices for an antihazing effort, we considered several additional research areas, including (1) hazing prevention and antihazing training, (2) general behavioral training, (3) bullying prevention and antibullying training, (4) violence prevention and antiviolence training, and (5) sexual assault prevention and anti–sexual assault training. After establishing a preliminary list of relevant studies based on our search terms, we reviewed the references listed within the studies to identify additional research. Finally, we asked informed colleagues to review our lists and identify research that might have been overlooked.

In determining what literature to include in our review, we limited ourselves to material published from January 1990 to June 2013, that was written in English, and that addressed behaviors among humans. We also included only research that involved quantitative or qualitative data collection, a description of a theoretical model, or a relatively comprehensive review of the literature. This excluded pure opinion pieces and book reviews.

Interviews with Hazing Subject-Matter Experts

We also conducted semistructured interviews with leading hazing researchers and prevention experts who have published books, articles, or reports relevant to hazing prevention and response. These interviews addressed several topics, including factors that contribute to the persistence of hazing, general efforts to reduce hazing, antihazing training, evaluation of hazing reduction efforts, and options for reporting hazing. Interviews lasted approximately 30 to 45 minutes. The information from these interviews complemented that found in our review of the literature. Thus, interviewee comments are noted throughout the chapters.

Subject-matter experts included the following:

- Hank Nuwer, author and conference speaker on hazing
- Jennifer Waldron, University of Northern Iowa
- Judy Van Raalte, Springfield College
- Caroline Keating, Colgate University
- Mary Madden, University of Maine
- R. Brian Crow, Slippery Rock University
- Charles Hall, HazingPrevention.Org
- Susan Lipkins, insidehazing.com
- Norm Pollard, Alfred University.

APPENDIX B

A Case Study in Hazing Reform

This appendix provides an in-depth description and discussion of an institutional hazing reform example. The 2011 hazing-related death of Robert Champion, a drum major at FAMU, prompted comprehensive reform of antihazing efforts at the university. Because this case involves reform at a civilian institution, not all the specific reforms at FAMU will be directly applicable to DoD. However, because this case illustrates major systemic reform (rather than individual corrective action), it may provide translatable lessons for instituting change within DoD at the system level.

In particular, this case study provides an example of the kind of organizational and personal efforts described in Chapter Four: systemwide approaches, accountability for leaders, and gaining culture-specific insight into local contextual factors that contribute to hazing. This case study also shows examples of organizational-level prevention efforts, such as reporting reform, and punishment efforts that include broadened responsibility for hazing reporting. Finally, the case study shows examples of reforms of person-level efforts to change knowledge, attitudes, and behavior and training reform based on sound pedagogy.

A Note on Sources

RAND research typically synthesizes many primary and secondary sources. However, case studies are narrow and targeted and, in this case, report on a single institution's response to a hazing crisis. This appendix draws from two primary sources: FAMU's Board of Trustees report to the Board of Governors, State University System of Florida, and discussion with the Special Assistant to the President for Anti-Hazing, who oversaw the reform efforts. Being able to discuss in-depth the context, challenges, and insights of the reform effort with the execution officer leveraged our understanding of the official written report.

Prior to Reform

The death of Robert Champion and subsequent investigation spurred major reform of antihazing policy and programs at FAMU. Champion was a drum major in FAMU's "Marching 100" band who willingly participated in a hazing ritual called "crossing over" in 2011. Champion walked a front-of-the-bus-to-the-back gauntlet while fellow band members beat and kicked him. Champion died of hemorrhagic shock due to soft tissue damage sustained during the beating. The death was ruled a homicide, and 11 band members were charged with manslaughter and felony hazing. The incident received widespread national attention, and severe scrutiny on the culture and practice of hazing at FAMU.

The IG's report on behalf of the Board of Governors shows that, prior to reform, there were serious inadequacies at the organizational and individual levels, particularly in terms of institutional controls, the reporting and tracking systems for infractions, and training and staffing of student organizations. A brief overview of these issues provides a context for better understanding the reform effort.

Institutional Controls

The investigation revealed that, at the organizational level, the institution lacked both the means and structure for institutional support of antihazing efforts. Middle-management staffing and funding were inadequate to pursue antihazing efforts, which was compounded by inadequate reporting and inadequate communication procedures between staff and senior leaders in the university. There was also a lack of oversight and supervision of collaboration and communication between student affairs and local law enforcement agencies.

University policy was also lacking. There were discrepancies between institutional documents, and there was no formal policy for many of the university's antihazing efforts (e.g., reporting, referral, responsibility, coordination with law enforcement). While there was antihazing education, there was no standard presentation and no documentation of delivery. Finally, the university's position on hazing was unclear; for example, the university had not articulated a "zero tolerance" policy toward hazing.

Another compounding factor was the lack of automated tracking systems for reports, investigations, and judicial outcomes, so that oversight depended on human attention. Reporting could thus not be tied directly to investigations and judicial action—human attention and memory were required to initiate and track a response. There were no written policies for referral of possible violations from campus police to judicial affairs—referral was ad hoc, based on staff members' judgments about the seriousness of potential violations—incidents involving bodily harm always received attention, ones without bodily harm might not.

Reporting Systems

The report also shows that, prior to reform, there were multiple barriers to effective reporting of possible hazing violations at FAMU. Existing reporting was not anonymous; did not include antiretaliation provisions; used a manual, paper-based system; and was oriented around more-formal reports to Judicial Affairs and external law enforcement. Also, there was no university policy designating who was required to report and to whom reports should be made. Furthermore, there were no university-mandated reporting periods for timely action on reporting or for any part of the referral system.

Student Organizations

The supervision, support, and guidance within student organizations was inadequate for deterring hazing. There were no suitable intake procedures for members and no dedicated compliance staff. Thus, prior to reform, ineligible individuals (i.e., nonstudents) were able to join student organizations. The investigation found that failing to vet members of student organizations, including allowing people who were not part of the university to join student organizations, contributed to the hazing culture at FAMU. There were also no educational requirements for membership in student organizations or for faculty advisors. Student organizations required only a single, untrained faculty advisor, who was not supervised or vetted by the institution, and there was no ongoing outreach to student organizations to ensure members understood and accepted university antihazing policy.

Systemic Failure

The above summary of the report's findings shows that hazing problems at FAMU were endemic to the system. There were gaps at both the organizational and individual levels; thus, hazing incidents, such as the Champion case, could not be dismissed as aberrations or simply individual misconduct. Instead, the university needed comprehensive antihazing reform.

Antihazing Reform

In the wake of Robert Champion's death and a formal investigation of FAMU's antihazing policy and efforts, the university undertook sweeping reform. Two sources identified gaps in FAMU's antihazing program: the Office of the Inspector General and Director of Compliance Antihazing Program Investigation report, and FAMU's internal research effort (which functioned as a needs assessment; Harper, 2012). This led to deliberate reform in which the component parts interlocked to create a coordinated effort across the organizational and individual levels. In studying this antihazing effort, we identified both organizational- and individual-level antihazing reforms, detailed in the following subsections.

Organizational-Level Change

Institutional Understanding of Hazing

As part of a deliberate and comprehensive antihazing reform effort, the university established an internal antihazing research initiative and reached out to student and community groups and other universities to gain a greater understanding of hazing practices and impact. The university also engaged in data analytics and discovered that performance groups, not just Greek organizations, were prone to hazing at FAMU, including dance troupes, modeling, and service organizations. The internal research effort determined that the reasons for this included cultural spread outward from Greek organizations through cross memberships and pointed to the need for universitywide antihazing efforts. Hazing could not be framed as solely a Greek organization or marching band problem.

The hazing research initiative also found qualitative differences between hazing at predominantly white institutions and historically black institutions. For example, alcohol is more implicated in hazing at predominantly white institutions. Because not all hazing contexts are alike, not every best practice or solution from the wider world of university governance would apply to a historically black institution, such as FAMU.

Intake and Membership Procedures for Student Organizations

The university established new criteria for intake procedures for all membership organizations, including antihazing certification as a prerequisite for membership. This means ensuring that prospective members are qualified for membership (i.e., actually enrolled students at the university, in good standing) and do not have pending investigations or adjudications that would preclude them from membership. Students also must take antihazing training and document their understanding of policy and commitment to compliance. Marching bands have a particular historical context and cultural importance in historically black institutions that has made them a locus for hazing, so FAMU established new assessment criteria for music scholarship recipients, including higher grade point average standards.

Parallel to this student effort, FAMU changed institutional hiring practices in positions of power in student organizations (e.g., Director of the Marching Band). FAMU added screening and employment criteria for hiring in positions of power in organizations, including expressed attitudes toward hazing and knowledge and experience in antihazing, reflecting a new institutional position that antihazing is an embedded responsibility for staff that lead student organizations.

Faculty Advisor System

Similar to the new hiring criteria for student organization leadership staff, FAMU established guidelines for faculty advisors of student organizations. FAMU instituted mandatory training and certification for all faculty advisors and added mandatory refresher training at the beginning of each semester. Thus, the faculty advisor system now has both built-in training at the front end and continuing education to maintain antihazing awareness and practice. Another important institutional staff change mandates a dual-advisor system for all student organizations and prohibitions against advisors being alone with students. This dual-advisor system is intended to provide an additional check on hazing practices because the advisors are jointly accountable to each other.

Internal and External Communication and Outreach

FAMU made comprehensive changes to its communication policy and practice, both in internal communication and in external coordination and outreach. The Tallahassee Police Department now sends weekly reports directly to both the FAMU Department of Public Safety and Judicial Affairs, and the university works with local law enforcement entities through established mutual aid agreements. In turn, the university communicates all allegations of hazing that occur off campus to the law enforcement entity having jurisdiction (i.e., Tallahassee Police Department, Leon County Sheriff's Office) and stays abreast of such cases throughout the investigation process.

As part of its internal antihazing communications strategy, the university established an antihazing website (FAMU, undated). There, students can get information on hazing in general and on specific university policy on hazing and can both reaffirm and document that they understand and will abide by the regulations. As part of its external outreach, FAMU has identified Florida high schools from which it regularly recruits and conducts hazing awareness at these schools to start changing attitudes and communicating university culture on hazing before students get to FAMU.

Adjudication and Enforcement

FAMU conducted a comprehensive assessment of punishments for hazing. This led to including restorative justice to the potential outcomes for hazers, e.g., having hazers teach antihazing. The university found that genuinely contrite offenders could offer great insight as former hazers and make persuasive trainers. Restorative justice efforts like this require distinguishing between those who show self-awareness and repentance and those who are defiant about their involvement in hazing.

Additionally, the university amended its antihazing policy to make willing participation in hazing a violation. As part of its research and reform effort, the university found that many victims of hazing actively desired the hazing as a legitimate test that validated their membership. Thus, prevention and punishment now include hazing participants, not just perpetrators. Finally, FAMU added "zero-tolerance" language to its policy and documents to make its stance against hazing explicit.

Investigations

Organizational-level reforms at the university also included improving the quality of investigations and coordinating investigations to match other elements of enforcement. FAMU instituted a parallel investigation system, one for Judicial Affairs (to ensure adherence to university policy) and one for Criminal Investigation (to ensure compliance with state law). Furthermore, the university general counsel is now included in all communications about hazing investigations as an additional check on the system.

In an attempt to balance a deliberate investigative process against the need to prevent additional hazing infractions, student membership groups with outstanding hazing allegations are placed on suspension until the allegations have been resolved but may petition for expedited hearings. There is also now a provision for expedited hearings for individuals deemed potential threats, as well as accommodations for suspects (e.g., remote classes, limited campus access). The purpose of these provisions is to keep potential perpetrators away from others they may harm or influence.

Oversight and Accountability

The university engaged in a substantial overhaul of organizational-level oversight and accountability systems. Key to this was researching and adopting tracking-system software to support oversight of reporting, investigation, and judicial action. Prior to reform, human-based tracking systems had meant that high-profile cases that involved bodily harm received adequate attention but that other incidents might be lost in the system. The university selected a software suite that allows selective visibility of reports, allows inclusion of written documents and notes, enhances the transfer of information between all agencies involved, and provides institution-wide analytics on student conduct.

An additional accountability measure was to amend the policy and practice of forwarding criminal incident reports to Judicial Affairs, now by using signed cover transmittal and receipt forms. The university also required all students to sign antihazing agreements (prior to reform, this was required only of members of the marching band). FAMU also required recertification of all student organizations on university antihazing policy. All these oversight reforms reflect the principle of a lower level of action, coupled with a higher level of oversight, meant to keep direct decisionmakers in the loop.

Staffing

Organizational-level reform also included changing staffing levels and structure. This included reorganizing the Office of Judicial Affairs and adding two new staff members, as well as reconstituting a defunct external antihazing committee, with a special assistant to the president as liaison. The Department of Music was reorganized, including the addition of a new compliance officer. At the highest level, the university created the position of special assistant to the president for antihazing. That antihazing officer is generally responsible for university antihazing efforts and has specific duties in assessing reporting and compliance, liaison with the university president, antihazing data analytics, monitoring student affairs in relation to hazing, drafting university correspondence about antihazing, and coordination of university and off-university partners in antihazing.

Reporting Systems

The reporting system was reformed to support participation. New provisions prohibit retaliation for reporting, and now all university employees are considered mandatory reporters. A new, online, anonymous hazing reporting system links to campus police to further bolster reporting. The system automatically alerts the Office of Judicial Affairs and the Anti-Hazing special assistant and creates an entry in the tracking system software.

The university revised its antihazing regulation to encourage and better support reporting, including a mandated 24-hour action deadline for all reporting steps. Under the new antihazing policy, all informational reports compiled from an alleged violation of the Student Code of Conduct occurring on or off campus are forwarded to the Office of Judicial Affairs within the next business day, unless extenuating circumstances prohibit this. All informational reports compiled from outside agency cases alleging students' criminal conduct off campus are also forwarded to the Office of Judicial Affairs within the next business day, unless extenuating circumstances prohibit this.

Individual-Level Change

Partnering with Alumni and National Organizations

The university leveraged connections with external organizations with aligned interests, enlisting their help in effecting culture change around hazing. One effort was partnering with national organizations (e.g., national Greek organizations) to enlist their aid in creating a no-hazing culture. Because of legal liability, national-level parent organizations have a high stake in preventing hazing, which makes them willing partners. The second line of effort was to partner with concerned alumni, leveraging their affiliation with the university to enlist their aid in changing culture and in communication and outreach, and trained alumni serve as antihazing education facilitators. Critical to this outreach was communicating to alumni that the institution they valued was at risk.

Pedagogical Reform

Pedagogical reform was critical to improving antihazing education. The university replaced large-group, lecture-style delivery of slide presentations with small discussion groups, finding that small-group antihazing discussions lead to more honesty and engagement from participants.

The university also enhanced the effectiveness of facilitators by selecting ones who would have ethos and credibility with students: other students, former hazers, and alumni who had participated in prestigious student organizations. The university also adopted a train-the-trainer approach to preparing hazing education facilitators, to seed antihazing knowledge among the student population. The university also found that conspiracy after the fact could be as serious a problem as the hazing incident itself. Thus, antihazing education seminars also include arguments against a cover-up culture.

Alternative Bonding Opportunities

While hazing is wrong in practice, the motivations behind it can include legitimate interests, such as building cohesion. To meet this legitimate need, the university followed best practices by offering safe and ethical sanctioned bonding opportunities. For example, philanthropic competitions have been used as a healthy way to orient and bond new students. The university has also created team-building activities to allow students in organizations to experience hardship and problem solving in a safe environment. This team-building exercise is based on the Leadership Reaction Course at USMC recruit training and offers a "Crucible-like" experience of having undergone a meaningful test but within a safe, supervised environment.

A Relevant Example for DoD

There are significant contextual differences between antihazing efforts at a civilian university and the U.S. military, but this civilian antihazing reform effort provides examples of many of the key principles and recommendations outlined in Chapter Four. Thus, while specific antihazing efforts may or may not be directly transferrable to a military setting, the whole can function as a kind of battle study from which lessons can be learned.

Most important, the antihazing effort at FAMU had two parallel lines of effort, at the organizational and individual levels. Organizational-level efforts improved communication and tracking, enhancing accountability and oversight. Organizational prevention efforts also meant staffing reform to include dedicated personnel to carry out and be accountable for antihazing efforts. At the individual level, antihazing efforts now include education and documentation to ensure that university members fully understand hazing policy. These educational efforts are tied to a broad and vigorous effort to change attitudes and perceptions and thus change behavior. Critical to both the education and attitudinal efforts was pedagogical reform that closely matches our recommendations.

These core lines of effort sprang from a needs assessment that identified gaps in existing efforts, so that reform could be deliberate, internally coordinated, and well designed in terms of matching effort to need. The internal review also led to a better understanding of the local context and contributing factors for hazing to facilitate more-effective efforts, particularly at the individual level. The FAMU case provides a clear example of how a needs assessment can guide an effort that is coordinated, comprehensive, and well designed.

Further, this case study may inspire innovative responses from the services. University leaders realized they had a powerful resource in their alumni, and leveraged that resource by communicating to alumni the risk the university faced. Similarly, the services have a committed alumni population of retirees and former members who may be situated to help effect culture change and perceptions about hazing. We also note that FAMU borrowed one of its alternative bonding activities from the USMC. No one knows more about building cohesion and providing meaningful tests for membership (in safe, structured ways) than the services. This institutional knowledge is a potentially powerful resource in directing junior members' desire to feel legitimacy as members, instead of through hazing.

APPENDIX C

Coding of Service-Level Hazing Prevention Training and Education

This appendix provides more detail on our coding of the hazing-relevant training materials the services provided us. Two RAND researchers developed a coding scheme to assist with rating the extent to which these materials provided evidence of factors, or categories, of interest. In coding the training material content, the following factors were addressed: hazing policy description, characteristics of hazing, example hazing acts, full DoD definition, how hazing is disciplined, how to report hazing, duty to report and/or address hazing, information on the negative effects of hazing, information on misperceptions about hazing, and critical thinking skills to assist with addressing hazing. In coding the training techniques used, the following factors were addressed: use of lecture, use of instructor-led discussion, use of structured assessment, and use of in-class activities. Tables C.1 and C.2 provide the codebook used for these factors. Information on the training structure was obtained through review of the materials and interviews with service representatives, and a coding scheme was not developed for this content.

Ratings of each factor were based on the frequency and detail of description of the factor within the provided training materials. After the development of a codebook, two individuals each independently coded all the training materials using the established coding scheme. After both individuals completed coding of the materials, intercoder reliability statistics were calculated. Results showed that intercoder agreement was substantial (kappa = 0.77; see Hrushka et al., 2004). Discrepancies in coding were addressed through discussion.

Table C.1
Codebook for Training Material Content

Training Characteristics	No Evidence	Limited Evidence	Moderate Evidence	A Great Deal of Evidence
Policy Description	No description of hazing policy in any provided materials	Provision of a short policy description in approximately less than half of the provided materials	Provision of a short policy description in most provided materials Provision of a thorough policy description in in approximately less than half of provided materials	Provision of a thorough policy description in approximately most or all provided materials
Characteristics of Hazing	No description of the characteristics of hazing in any provided materials	Provision of limited description of a few hazing characteristics in most provided materials No description of characteristics in some materials and a limited description in all other provided materials	Provision of lengthier description of hazing characteristics in approximately less than half of provided materials	Thorough description of several characteristics of hazing in most or all provided materials
Example Hazing Acts	No provision of hazing examples in any provided materials	Provision of very few examples in all or most provided materials	Provision of several examples in most provided materials Thorough description of multiple examples in approximately less than half of provided materials	Thorough description of multiple examples in most provided materials

Table C.1—Continued

Training Characteristics	No Evidence	Limited Evidence	Moderate Evidence	A Great Deal of Evidence
Full DoD definition	No provision of the 1997 DoD definition of hazing in any provided materials Provision of either unrelated definition of hazing or no definition in most provided materials	Provision of parts of DoD definition in most provided materials Provision of either parts of DoD definition or similar service definition in most provided materials	Provision of the full 1997 DoD definition with examples in approximately less than half of provided materials	Provision of the full 1997 DoD definition with examples in most or all provided materials
How hazing disciplined	No description of disciplinary actions or policies regarding hazing in any provided materials	Limited general discussion of UCMJ in relation to hazing in some provided materials	Limited discussion of UCMJ or other penalties in relation to hazing in all or most provided materials	Thorough description of UCMJ and other penalties in most or all provided materials
How to report	No description of reporting options in any provided materials	Provision of limited reporting options in all or most of provided materials Provision of several reporting options in approximately less than half of materials and limited or no reporting options in other materials	Provision of several reporting options in all or most provided materials	Provision of multiple reporting options, including specific contact numbers and/or email addresses, in all or most provided materials
Duty to report or address	No description of personal responsibility to report or address hazing in any provided materials	Provision of limited description of responsibility to address hazing in all or most of provided materials	Thorough description of individual responsibility to address hazing in approximately less than half of provided materials	Thorough description of individual responsibility to address hazing in most or all provided materials

Table C.1—Continued

Training Characteristics	No Evidence	Limited Evidence	Moderate Evidence	A Great Deal of Evidence
Awareness: negative effects	No description of the negative mental, physical, or career effects of hazing in any provided materials	Provision of limited description of negative consequences in approximately less than half of provided materials	Provision of more-detailed description regarding general negative consequences in all or most provided materials	Provision of thorough description of how hazing can lead to multiple, specific consequences in all provided materials
Awareness: misperceptions	No description of myths or incorrect beliefs regarding hazing in any provided materials	Provision of limited description of misperceptions in approximately less than half of provided materials	Provision of more-detailed description of general misperceptions in most provided materials Provision of limited description of misperceptions in approximately less than half of provided materials	Provision of thorough description of multiple, specific misperceptions in all provided materials
Skills (e.g., critical thinking)	No discussion of cognitive skills or leadership skills involved in addressing hazing in any provided materials	Provision of limited discussion of cognitive and/or leadership skills in less than half of provided materials—must be beyond a few actions to take	Provision of more-detailed discussion of cognitive and/or leadership skills in most provided materials—must be beyond a few actions to take	Provision of thorough discussion of cognitive and leadership skills that are specifically applicable to addressing hazing—must be beyond a few actions to take

Table C.2
Codebook for Training Techniques

Training Characteristics	No Evidence	Limited Evidence	Moderate Evidence	A Great Deal of Evidence
Lecture	No provision of lecture-based information in any provided materials	Evidence of lecture in approximately less than half of provided materials	Evidence of lecture in approximately half of provided materials	Evidence of lecture in all or most provided materials
Instructor-led discussion	No mention of instructor-led discussion in any provided materials	Evidence of instructor-led class discussion in approximately less than half of provided materials	Evidence of instructor-led class discussion in approximately half of provided materials	Evidence of instructor-led class discussion in all or most provided materials
Structured assessment	No provision of a written exam or quiz assessing hazing knowledge in any provided materials	Provision of a limited written assessment of general negative workplace behaviors at the end of any provided materials	Provision of a limited written assessment of hazing knowledge specifically at the end of any provided materials	Provision of a comprehensive written assessment of hazing knowledge specifically at the end of most provided materials
In-class activities[a]	No mention of class-based discussion or class activities in any provided materials	Evidence of limited class-based discussion in most materials Or evidence of limited class-based discussion in some materials and no discussion in remaining materials	Evidence of thorough class-based discussion in approximately less than half of materials	Evidence of thorough class-based discussion in most materials

[a] Class activities are those that are not entirely led by an instructor.

References

10 USC 47, Uniform Code of Military Justice.

Ajzen, Icek, "The Theory of Planned Behavior," *Organizational Behavior and Human Decision Processes,* Vol. 50, No. 2, December 1991, pp. 179–211.

Allan, Elizabeth J., and Mary Madden, *Hazing in View: College Students at Risk,* Orono, Me.: University of Maine, March 11, 2008. As of August 5, 2014: http://umaine.edu/hazingresearch/files/2012/10/hazing_in_view_web.pdf

Aronson, Elliot, and Judson Mills, "The Effects of Severity of Initiation on Liking for a Group," *Journal of Abnormal and Social Psychology,* Vol. 59, No. 2, September 1959, pp. 177–181.

Atkinson, Quentin D., and Harvey Whitehouse, "The Cultural Morphospace of Ritual Form: Examining Modes of Religiosity Cross-Culturally," *Evolution and Human Behavior,* Vol. 32, No. 1, January 2011, pp. 50–62.

Baumeister, Roy F., and Mark R. Leary, "The Need to Belong: Desire for Interpersonal Attachments as a Fundamental Human Motivation," *Psychological Bulletin,* Vol. 117, No. 3, May 1995, pp. 497–529.

Bingham, Shereen G., and Lisa L. Scherer, "The Unexpected Effects of a Sexual Harassment Educational Program," *Journal of Applied Behavioral Science,* Vol. 37, No. 2, June 2001, pp. 125–153.

Bond, Lynne A., and Amy M. Carmola Hauf, "Community-Based Collaboration: An Overarching Best Practice in Prevention," *The Counseling Psychologist,* Vol. 35, No. 4, July 2007, pp. 567–575.

Burke, Lisa A., and Holly M. Hutchins, "Training Transfer: An Integrative Literature Review," *Human Resource Development Review,* Vol. 6, No. 3, September 2007, pp. 263–296.

Crano, William D., and Radmilla Prislin, eds., *Attitudes and Attitude Change,* New York: Psychology Press, 2008.

Cimino, Aldo, "The Evolution of Hazing: Motivational Mechanisms and the Abuse of Newcomers," *Journal of Cognition and Culture,* Vol. 11, Nos. 3–4, 2011, pp. 241–267.

Cimino, Aldo, and Andrew W. Delton, "On the Perceptions of Newcomers: Toward an Evolved Psychology of Intergenerational Coalitions," *Human Nature,* Vol. 21, No. 2, June 2010, pp. 186–202.

Cohen, William A., "Hazing," memorandum for the Secretaries of the Military Departments et al., Washington, D.C.: U.S. Department of Defense, August 28, 1997.

Crow, R. Brian, and Eric W. Macintosh. "Conceptualizing a Meaningful Definition of Hazing in Sport," *European Sport Management Quarterly,* Vol. 9, No. 4, 2009, pp. 433–451.

Crow, R. Brian, and Scott R. Rosner, "Institutional and Organizational Liability for Hazing in Intercollegiate and Professional Team Sports," *St. John's Law Review,* Vol. 76, No. 1, Winter 2002, pp. 87–114.

Crow, Brian, Robin Ammon, and Dennis R. Phillips, "Anti-Hazing Strategies for Coaches and Administrators," *Strategies: A Journal for Physical and Sports Educators,* Vol. 17, No. 4, 2013, pp. 13–15.

Daniels, Robert A., "Illicit Initiations and Ritual Ambiguity in the 82nd Airborne," presented at the Annual Meeting of the Society for Cross-Cultural Research, Santa Fe, N.M., February 28, 1992.

Defense Equal Opportunity Management Institute, *DEOMI Organizational Climate Survey (DEOCS),* website, undated. As of April 2, 2014: http://www.deocs.net/public/index.cfm

Deslauriers, Louis, Ellen Schelew, and Carl Wieman,"Improved Learning in a Large-Enrollment Physics Class," *Science,* Vol. 332, No. 6031, May 13, 2011, pp. 862–864.

Dick, Walter, and Lou Carey, *The Systematic Design of Instruction,* New York: Harper Collins Publishers, 1990.

Directive-Type Memorandum 08-049, "Recovery Coordination Program: Improvements to the Care, Management, and Transition of Recovering Service Members (RSMs)," Washington, D.C.: Office of the Under Secretary of Defense for Personnel and Readiness, January 19, 2009.

Dixon, Melissa, "Hazing in High Schools: Ending the Hidden Tradition," *Journal of Law and Education,* Vol. 30, No. 2, April 2001, pp. 356–363.

Dornbusch, Sanford M., "The Military Academy as an Assimilating Institution," *Social Forces,* Vol. 33, No. 4, May 1955, pp. 316–321.

Driscoll, Marcy P., *Psychology of Learning for Instruction,* 2nd ed., Boston: Allyn & Bacon Publishers, 2000.

Dunham, Richard M., Jeannie S. Kidwell, and Stephen M. Wilson, "Rites of Passage at Adolescence: A Ritual Process Paradigm," *Journal of Adolescent Research,* Vol. 1, No. 2, Summer 1986, pp. 139–153.

Dutton, Donald G., and Susan Painter, "Emotional Attachments in Abusive Relationships: A Test of Traumatic Bonding Theory," *Violence and Victims*, Vol. 8, No. 2, 1993, pp. 105–120.

Edelman, Marc, "How to Prevent High School Hazing: A Legal, Ethical, and Social Primer," *North Dakota Law Review*, Vol. 81, Fall 2005, pp. 309–341.

Ellsworth, Chad William, *Definitions of Hazing: Differences among Selected Student Organizations*, thesis, College Park: University of Maryland, 2004.

FAMU—*See* Florida Agricultural and Mechanical University.

Ferdman, Bernardo M., and Sari Eny Brody, "Models of Diversity Training," in Dan Landis and Rabi S. Bhagat, eds., *Handbook of Intercultural Training*, 2nd ed., Thousand Oaks, Calif.: Sage, 1996, pp. 282–303.

Fields, Sarah K., Christy L. Collins, and R. Dawn Comstock, "Conflict on the Courts: A Review of Sports-Related Violence Literature," *Trauma, Violence, & Abuse*, Vol. 8, No. 4, October 2007, pp. 359–369.

Finkel, Michelle A., "Traumatic Injuries Caused by Hazing Practices," *American Journal of Emergency Medicine,* Vol. 20, No. 3, May 2002, pp. 228–233.

FIPG—*See* Fraternity Insurance Purchasing Group.

Florida Agricultural and Mechanical University, Committed to Ending Hazing, website, undated. As of August 22, 2014:
http://www.famu.edu/hazing/

Florida Agricultural and Mechanical University Board of Trustees, *Response to Preliminary Report of Investigation Regarding FAMU's Pre-2012 Anti-Hazing Program*, Tallahassee, Fla., 2013. As of July 22, 2014:
http://www.famu.edu/OfficeofCommunications/FINAL%20Response%20for%20BOG.pdf

Fisher, Bonnie S., "The Effects of Survey Question Wording on Rape Estimates Evidence from a Quasi-Experimental Design," *Violence Against Women*, Vol. 15, No. 2, February 2009, pp. 133–147.

Fraternity Insurance Purchasing Group, Inc., *Risk Management Manual*, Indianapolis, Ind., 2008.

GAO—*See* U.S. Government Accountability Office.

Garamone, Jim, "Rite of Passage," American Forces Press Service, no date. As of October 10, 2014:
http://www.defense.gov/specials/basic/

Glionna, John M., "Midshipman Recalls Her Rough Seas at Annapolis: Harassment," *Los Angeles Times*, May 23, 1990. As of October 20, 2014:
http://articles.latimes.com/1990-05-23/local/me-86_1_naval-academy

Groah, J. S., *Treatment of Fourth Class Midshipmen: Hazing and Its Impact on Academic and Military Performance and Psychological and Physical Health*, dissertation, Monterey, Calif.: Naval Postgraduate School, 2005.

Gump, Brooks B., and James A. Kulik, "Stress, Affiliation, and Emotional Contagion," *Journal of Personality and Social Psycology*, Vol. 72, No. 2, February 1997, pp. 305–391.

Hage, Sally M., John L. Romano, Robert K. Conyne, Maureen Kenny, Connie Matthews, Jonathan P. Schwartz, and Michael Waldo, "Best Practice Guidelines on Prevention Practice, Research, Training, and Social Advocacy for Psychologists," *The Counseling Psychologist*, Vol. 35, No. 4, July 2007, pp. 493–566.

Harmon-Jones, Eddie, and Cindy Harmon-Jones, "Cognitive Dissonance Theory After 50 Years of Development," *Zeitschrift für Sozialpsychologie*, Vol. 38, 2007, pp. 7–16.

Harper, Derry, *The Florida A&M University Anti-Hazing Program: Preliminary Report of Investigation*, State University System of Florida Board of Governors, December 28, 2012. As of August 22, 2014: http://www.flbog.edu/documents_meetings/0175_0661_5225_206%20AUD%203b_BOG_OIGC_2011-038_Final.pdf

Henrich, Joseph, "The Evolution of Costly Displays, Cooperation and Religion: Credibility Enhancing Displays and Their Implications for Cultural Evolution," *Evolution and Human Behavior*, Vol. 30, No. 4, July 2009, pp. 244–260.

Hollman, Barbara B., "Hazing: Hidden Campus Crime," *New Directions for Student Services*, No. 99, Fall 2002, pp. 11–23.

Hoover, Nadine C., *Initiation Rites and Athletics: A National Survey of NCAA Sports Teams*, Alfred, N.Y.: Alfred University, 1999.

Hoover, Nadine C., and Norman J. Pollard, *Initiation Rites in American High Schools: A National Survey*, Alfred, N.Y.: Alfred University, 2000.

Hruschka, Daniel J., Deborah Schwartz, Daphne Cobb St. John, Erin Picone-Decaro, Richard A. Jenkins, and James W. Carey, "Reliability in Coding Open-Ended Data: Lessons Learned from HIV Behavioral Research," *Field Methods*, Vol. 16, No. 3, August 2004, pp. 307–331.

Johnson, Jay, "Across the Threshold: A Comparative Analysis of Communitas and Rites of Passage in Sport Hazing and Initiations," *Canadian Journal of Sociology*, Vol. 36, No. 3, 2011, pp. 199–228.

Johnson, Jay, and Margery Holman, *Making the Team: Inside the World of Sport Hazing and Initiations*, Toronto: Canadian Scholars' Press, 2004.

Kalev, Alexandra, Erin Kelly, and Frank Dobbin, "Best Practices or Best Guesses? Assessing the Efficacy of Corporate Affirmative Action and Diversity Policies," *American Sociological Review*, Vol. 71, August 2006, pp. 589–617.

Keating, Caroline F., Jason Pomerantz, Stacy D. Pommer, Samantha J. H. Ritt, Lauren M. Miller, and Julie McCormick, "Going to College and Unpacking Hazing: A Functional Approach to Decrypting Initiation Practices Among Undergraduates," *Group Dynamics: Theory, Research, and Practice*, Vol. 9, No. 2, 2005, pp. 104–126.

Kirkpatrick, Donald, "Great Ideas Revisited," *Training & Development*, Vol. 50, No. 1, January 1996, pp. 54–59.

Kittle, Paul Robert, *Assessing the Efficacy of Analytical Definitions of Hazing Education*, dissertation, Auburn, Ala.: Auburn University, 2012.

Koenig, Laura B., and Thomas J. Bouchard, Jr., "Genetic and Environmental Influences of the Traditional Moral Values Triad—Authoritarianism, Conservatism, and Religiousness—as Assessed by Quantitative Behavior Genetic Methods," in Patrick McNamara, ed., *Where God and Science Meet: Evolution, Genes, and the Religious Brain,* Westport, Conn.: Greenwood Publishing, 2006, pp. 31–61.

Kozaryn, Linda D., "Pentagon Leaders Outraged by Hazing," press release, Washington, D.C.: U.S. Department of Defense, Armed Forces Press Service, February 4, 1997. As of October 20, 2014:
http://www.defense.gov/news/newsarticle.aspx?id=40916

Kulik, Carol T., and Loriann Roberson, "Common Goals and Golden Opportunities: Evaluations of Diversity Education in Academic and Organization Settings," *Academy of Management Learning and Education*, Vol. 7, No. 3, September 2008, pp. 309–331.

Langford, Linda, "A Comprehensive Approach to Hazing Prevention in Higher Education Settings," working paper, Newton, Mass.: Higher Education Center for Alcohol and Other Drug Abuse and Violence Prevention, May 23, 2008.

Levine, David K., and Salvatore Modica, "Peer Discipline and Incentives Within Groups," paper, July 29, 2014. As of October 10, 2014:
http://levl104.wustl.edu/papers/peerdiscipline-new.pdf

Levine, John M., and Richard L. Moreland, "Group Socialization: Theory and Research," *European Journal of Social Psychology,* Vol. 5, No. 1, 1994, pp. 305–336.

Lewis, Darryll M. Halcomb, "The Criminalization of Fraternity, Non-Fraternity, and Non-Collegiate Hazing," *Mississippi Law Journal,* Vol. 61, 1991, pp. 111–156.

Liewer, Steve, "Navy Veteran Combats 'Don't Ask, Don't Tell,'" *San Diego Union Tribune*, October 21, 2009. As of October 31, 2014:
http://www.utsandiego.com/news/2009/oct/21/navy-vet-combats-8216dont-ask-dont-tell8217/2/?zIndex#article-copy

Lipkins, Susan, *Preventing Hazing: How Parents, Teachers, and Coaches Can Stop the Violence, Harassment, and Humiliation,* San Francisco, Calif.: Jossey-Bass, 2006.

Lodewijkx, Hein M., and Joseph E. M. M. Syroit, "Severity of Initiation Revisited: Does Severity of Initiation Increase Attractiveness in Real Groups?" *European Journal of Social Psychology*, Vol. 27, No. 3, May 1997, pp. 275–300.

Los Angeles Police Deparment, *Manual: The Los Angeles Police Department*, Los Angeles, Calif., 2013. As of September 3, 2013:
http://www.lapdonline.org/lapd_manual/

Manzanedo, A., *The Persistence of Hazing in the Military*, Quantico Va.: Marine Corps Command and Staff College, 2013.

Marcellino, William M., "Talk Like a Marine: USMC Linguistic Acculturation and Civil-Military Argument," *Discourse Studies*, Vol. 16, No. 3, 2013, pp. 1–21.

Marine Corps Order 1700.28B, "Hazing," May 20, 2013.

McIntyre, Jamie, "Pentagon Brass 'Disgusted' by Marine Hazing Ceremony," CNN, January 31, 1997. As of October 20, 2014:
http://www.cnn.com/US/9701/31/hazing/

Melchior, LTC Robert J., "307th Engineer Battalion Prop Blast: An Airborne Tradition," paper, Carlisle, Pa.: U.S. Army War College, 1991.

Montague, David R., Israt Tusty Zohra, Sonja L. Love, and Darryl K. McGee, "Hazing Typologies: Those Who Criminally Haze and Those Who Receive Criminal Hazing," *Victims and Offenders*, Vol. 3, No. 2–3, 2008, pp. 258–274.

National Collegiate Athletic Association, *Building New Traditions: Hazing Prevention in College Athletics*, Indianapolis, 2007. As of June 26, 2015:
http://www.ncaa.org/sites/default/files/hazing%20prevention%20handbook%20
57315.pdf

National Defense Authorization Act for Fiscal Year 2008.

National Defense Authorization Act for Fiscal Year 2009.

National Defense Authorization Act for Fiscal Year 2013.

NCAA—*See* National Collegiate Athletic Association.

Ni, Ching-Cahing, "Lance Cpl. Harry Lew, 21, of Santa Clara; Killed in Afghanistan," *Los Angeles Times*, July 10, 2011. As of October 5, 2014:
http://articles.latimes.com/2011/jul/10/local/la-me-harry-lew-20110710

Nicoletti, John, Sally Spencer-Thomas, and Christopher Bollinger, *Violence Goes to College: The Authoritative Guide to Prevention and Intervention*, Springfield, Ill.: Charles C. Thomas Publisher LTD, 2001.

Nuwer, Hank, *Wrongs of Passage: Fraternities, Sororities, Hazing, and Binge Drinking*, Bloomington, Ind.: Indiana University Press, 2001.

———, ed., *The Hazing Reader,* Bloomington, Ind.: Indiana University Press, 2004.

Office of the Deputy Assistant Secretary of Defense, *2013 Demographics Profile of the Military Community*, Washington, D.C., 2014.

Ostvik, Kristina, and Floyd Rudmin, "Bullying and Hazing Among Norwegian Army Soldiers: Two Studies of Prevalence, Context, and Cognition," *Military Psychology,* Vol. 13, No. 1, 2001, pp. 17–39.

Pelletier, Amie, "Regulation of Rites: The Effect and Enforcement of Current Anti-Hazing Statutes," *New England Journal on Criminal and Civil Confinement,* Vol. 28, Summer 2002, pp. 377–414.

Pendry, Louise F., Denise M. Driscoll, and Susannah C. T. Field, "Diversity Training: Putting Theory into Practice," *Journal of Occupational and Organizational Psychology*, Vol. 80, No. 1, March 2007, pp. 27–50.

Pershing, Jana L., "Men and Women's Experiences with Hazing in a Male-Dominated Elite Military Institution," *Men and Masculinities*, Vol. 8, No. 4, April 2006, pp. 470–492.

Prislin, Radmilla, and William D. Crano, "Attitudes and Attitude Change: The Fourth Peak," in Crano and Prislin, 2008, pp. 3–18.

Regan, Kayla, "Three Hutchinson High School Students Arrested in Alleged Branding Incident," *Wichita Eagle,* November 2, 2013. As of October 16, 2014: http://www.kansas.com/news/article1126787.html

Richardson, Brian K., Zuoming Wang, and Camille A. Hall, "Blowing the Whistle Against Greek Hazing: The Theory of Reasoned Action as a Framework for Reporting Intentions," *Communication Studies,* Vol. 63, No. 2, 2012, pp. 172–193.

Rocha, Joseph, "'Don't Ask, Don't Tell' Didn't Protect Me from Abuse in the Navy," *Washington Post,* October 11, 2009.

Salo, Mikael, and Guy L. Siebold, "Variables Impacting Peer Group Cohesion in the Finnish Conscript Service," *Journal of Political and Military Sociology*, Vol. 36, No. 1, June 2008, pp. 1–18.

Schopler, John, and Nicholas Bateson, "A Dependence Interpretation of the Effects of a Severe Initiation," *Journal of Personality,* Vol. 30, No. 4, December 1962, pp. 633–649.

Schultz, P. Wesley, Jennifer J. Tabanico, and Tania Rendon, "Normative Beliefs as Agents of Influence: Basic Processes and Real-World Applications," in Crano and Prislin, 2008, pp. 385–409.

Simon, Mallory, "Witnesses: FAMU Drum Major Beaten with Drum Mallets in Hazing Gauntlet," CNN, May 25, 2012. As of October 16, 2014: http://www.cnn.com/2012/05/24/justice/famu-hazing-documents/

Sosis, Richard, "The Adaptive Value of Religious Ritual Rituals," *American Scientist,* Vol. 92, No. 2, March–April 2004, pp. 166–172.

Sosis, Richard, and Bradley J. Ruffle, "Religious Ritual and Cooperation: Testing for a Relationship on Israeli Religious and Secular Kibbutzim," *Current Anthropology,* Vol. 44, No. 5, December 2003, pp. 713–722.

Sosis, Richard, Howard C. Kress, and James S. Boster, "Scars for War: Evaluating Alternative Signaling Explanations for Cross-Cultural Variance in Ritual Costs," *Evolution and Human Behavior*, Vol. 28, No. 4, July 2007, pp. 234–247.

Stone, Jeff, and Nicole C. Fernandez, "How Behavior Shapes Attitudes: Cognitive Dissonance Processes," in Crano and Prislin, 2008, pp. 313–336.

Stoudt, Brett G., "'You're Either In or You're Out': School Violence, Peer Discipline, and the (Re)Production of Hegemonic Masculinity," *Men and Masculinities*, Vol. 8, No. 3, January 2006, pp. 273–287.

Sweet, Stephen, "Understanding Fraternity Hazing," in Nuwer, 2004, pp. 1–13.

Tjaden, Patricia, and Nancy Thoennes, "Prevalence, Incidence, and Consequences of Violence Against Women: Findings from the National Violence Against Women Survey," research brief, Washington, D.C.: National Institute of Justice and Centers for Disease Control and Prevention, November 1998.

U.S. Air Force, *Hazing in the Armed Forces*, July 2013.

U.S. Department of Defense, *DoD SAPR Data Collection & Reporting System Concept Design Report*, Washington, D.C., 2009.

U.S. Marine Corps, 2nd Marine Division (Fwd), "Command Investigation Into the Line of Duty/Misconduct Determination in the Case of Lance Corporal Harry Lew," Regimental Combat Team 1 SJA 5800, April 30, 2011. As of October 10, 2014:
https://timemilitary.files.wordpress.com/2011/09/lew-rpt.pdf

U.S. Navy, "Command Investigation of the Facts and Circumstances of Surrounding Allegations Within the WMD Division of Naval Security Force Bahrain," January 16, 2007. As of October 10, 2014:
http://web.archive.org/web/20120912123924/http://www.youthradio.org/files/JCR/cpt1_13.pdf

U.S. Government Accountability Office,[1] *DoD Service Academies: More Changes Needed to Eliminate Hazing*, Washington, D.C., GAO/NSIAD-93-36, November 1992.

Valente, Thomas W., Patricia Peredes, and Patricia R. Poppe, "Matching the Message to the Process: The Relative Ordering of Knowledge, Attitudes, and Practices in Behavior Change Research," *Human Communications Research,* Vol. 24, No. 3, March 1998, pp. 366–385.

---

[1] Known at the time as the U.S. General Accounting Office.

Van Gennep, Arnold, *The Rites of Passage*, trans. Monika B. Vizedom and Gabrielle L. Caffee, Chicago: University of Chicago Press, 1960.

Van Raalte, Judy L., Allen E. Cornelius, Darwyn E. Linder, and Britton W. Brewer, "The Relationship Between Hazing and Team Cohesion," *Journal of Sport Behavior*, Vol. 30, No. 4, December 2007, pp. 491–507.

Vreeman, Rachel C., and Aaron E. Carroll, "A Systematic Review of School-Based Interventions to Prevent Bullying," *Archives of Pediatric Adolescent Medicine,* Vol. 161, No. 1, January 2007, pp. 78–88.

Waldron, Jennifer J., "A Social Norms Approach to Hazing Prevention Workshops," *Journal of Sport Psychology in Action,* Vol. 3, No. 1, 2012, pp. 12–20.

Waldron, Jennifer J., and Christopher L. Kowalski, "Crossing the Line: Rites of Passage, Team Aspects, and Ambiguity of Hazing," *Research Quarterly for Exercise and Sport*, Vol. 80, No. 2, June 2009, pp. 291–302.

Waldron, Jennifer J., Quinten Lynn, and Vikki Krane, "Duct Tape, Icy Hot & Paddles: Narratives of Initiation onto US Male Sport Teams," *Sport, Education, and Society,* Vol. 16, No. 1, January 2011, pp. 111–125.

Wandersman, Abraham, "Four Keys to Success (Theory, Implementation, Evaluation, and Resource/System Support): High Hopes and Challenges in Participation," *American Journal of Community Psychology,* Vol. 43, Nos. 1–2, March 2009, pp. 3–21.

Whitehouse, Harvey, *Inside the Cult: Religious Innovation and Transmission in Papua New Guinea*, New York: Oxford University Press, 1995.

———, "Rites of Terror: Emotion, Metaphor, and Memory in Melanesian Initiation Cults," *Journal of the Royal Anthropological Institute,* Vol. 2, No. 4, December 1996, pp. 703–715.

———, "Human Rites," *Aeon Magazine,* 2012. As of July 18, 2014: http://aeon.co/magazine/being-human/harvey-whitehouse-ritual/

Winslow, Donna, "Rites of Passage and Group Bonding in the Canadian Airborne," *Armed Forces and Society,* Vol. 25, No. 3, Spring 1999, pp. 429–457.

Zezima, Katie. "7 Students Pledging a Fraternity Are Burned," *New York Times,* November 21, 2008. As of October 16, 2014: http://www.nytimes.com/2008/11/22/us/22hazing.html